וְאָתָא הַשּׁוֹחֵט וְשָׁחַט לְתוֹרָא, דְּשָׁתָה לְמַיָּא, דְּכָבָה לְנוּרָא, דְּשָׂרַף לְחֻטְרָא, דְּהִכָּה לְכַלְבָּא, דְּנָשַׁךְ לְשֻׁנְרָא, דְּאָכְלָה לְגַדְיָא, דְּזַבִּין אַבָּא בִּתְרֵי זוּזֵי. חַד גַּדְיָא, חַד גַּדְיָא.

וְאָתָא מַלְאַךְ הַמָּוֶת וְשָׁחַט לְשׁוֹחֵט, דְּשָׁחַט לְתוֹרָא, דְּשָׁתָה לְמַיָּא, דְּכָבָה לְנוּרָא, דְּשָׂרַף לְחֻטְרָא, דְּהִכָּה לְכַלְבָּא, דְּנָשַׁךְ לְשֻׁנְרָא, דְּאָכְלָה לְגַדְיָא, דְּזַבִּין אַבָּא בִּתְרֵי זוּזֵי. חַד גַּדְיָא, חַד גַּדְיָא.

וְאָתָא הַקָּדוֹשׁ בָּרוּךְ הוּא וְשָׁחַט לְמַלְאַךְ הַמָּוֶת, דְּשָׁחַט לְשׁוֹחֵט, דְּשָׁחַט לְתוֹרָא, דְּשָׁתָה לְמַיָּא, דְּכָבָה לְנוּרָא, דְּשָׂרַף לְחֻטְרָא, דְּהִכָּה לְכַלְבָּא, דְּנָשַׁךְ לְשֻׁנְרָא, דְּאָכְלָה לְגַדְיָא, דְּזַבִּין אַבָּא בִּתְרֵי זוּזֵי. חַד גַּדְיָא, חַד גַּדְיָא.

נרצה

חַד גַּדְיָא, חַד גַּדְיָא

דְּזַבִּין אַבָּא בִּתְרֵי זוּזֵי, חַד גַּדְיָא, חַד גַּדְיָא. וְאָתָא שֻׁנְרָא וְאָכְלָה לְגַדְיָא, דְּזַבִּין אַבָּא בִּתְרֵי זוּזֵי. חַד גַּדְיָא, חַד גַּדְיָא.

וְאָתָא כַלְבָּא וְנָשַׁךְ לְשֻׁנְרָא, דְּאָכְלָה לְגַדְיָא, דְּזַבִּין אַבָּא בִּתְרֵי זוּזֵי. חַד גַּדְיָא, חַד גַּדְיָא.

וְאָתָא חֻטְרָא וְהִכָּה לְכַלְבָּא, דְּנָשַׁךְ לְשֻׁנְרָא, דְּאָכְלָה לְגַדְיָא, דְּזַבִּין אַבָּא בִּתְרֵי זוּזֵי. חַד גַּדְיָא, חַד גַּדְיָא.

וְאָתָא נוּרָא וְשָׂרַף לְחֻטְרָא, דְּהִכָּה לְכַלְבָּא, דְּנָשַׁךְ לְשֻׁנְרָא, דְּאָכְלָה לְגַדְיָא, דְּזַבִּין אַבָּא בִּתְרֵי זוּזֵי. חַד גַּדְיָא, חַד גַּדְיָא.

וְאָתָא מַיָּא וְכָבָה לְנוּרָא, דְּשָׂרַף לְחֻטְרָא, דְּהִכָּה לְכַלְבָּא, דְּנָשַׁךְ לְשֻׁנְרָא, דְּאָכְלָה לְגַדְיָא, דְּזַבִּין אַבָּא בִּתְרֵי זוּזֵי. חַד גַּדְיָא, חַד גַּדְיָא.

וְאָתָא תוֹרָא וְשָׁתָה לְמַיָּא, דְּכָבָה לְנוּרָא, דְּשָׂרַף לְחֻטְרָא, דְּהִכָּה לְכַלְבָּא, דְּנָשַׁךְ לְשֻׁנְרָא, דְּאָכְלָה לְגַדְיָא, דְּזַבִּין אַבָּא בִּתְרֵי זוּזֵי. חַד גַּדְיָא, חַד גַּדְיָא.

Nirtza

תִּשְׁעָה יַרְחֵי לֵדָה, שְׁמוֹנָה יְמֵי מִילָה, שִׁבְעָה יְמֵי שַׁבַּתָּא, שִׁשָּׁה סִדְרֵי מִשְׁנָה, חֲמִשָּׁה חֻמְשֵׁי תוֹרָה, אַרְבַּע אִמָּהוֹת, שְׁלֹשָׁה אָבוֹת, שְׁנֵי לֻחוֹת הַבְּרִית, אֶחָד אֱלֹהֵינוּ שֶׁבַּשָּׁמַיִם וּבָאָרֶץ.

אַחַד עָשָׂר מִי יוֹדֵעַ? אַחַד עָשָׂר אֲנִי יוֹדֵעַ: אַחַד עָשָׂר כּוֹכְבַיָּא, עֲשָׂרָה דִבְּרַיָּא, תִּשְׁעָה יַרְחֵי לֵדָה, שְׁמוֹנָה יְמֵי מִילָה, שִׁבְעָה יְמֵי שַׁבַּתָּא, שִׁשָּׁה סִדְרֵי מִשְׁנָה, חֲמִשָּׁה חֻמְשֵׁי תוֹרָה, אַרְבַּע אִמָּהוֹת, שְׁלֹשָׁה אָבוֹת, שְׁנֵי לֻחוֹת הַבְּרִית, אֶחָד אֱלֹהֵינוּ שֶׁבַּשָּׁמַיִם וּבָאָרֶץ.

שְׁנֵים עָשָׂר מִי יוֹדֵעַ? שְׁנֵים עָשָׂר אֲנִי יוֹדֵעַ: שְׁנֵים עָשָׂר שִׁבְטַיָּא, אַחַד עָשָׂר כּוֹכְבַיָּא, עֲשָׂרָה דִבְּרַיָּא, תִּשְׁעָה יַרְחֵי לֵדָה, שְׁמוֹנָה יְמֵי מִילָה, שִׁבְעָה יְמֵי שַׁבַּתָּא, שִׁשָּׁה סִדְרֵי מִשְׁנָה, חֲמִשָּׁה חֻמְשֵׁי תוֹרָה, אַרְבַּע אִמָּהוֹת, שְׁלֹשָׁה אָבוֹת, שְׁנֵי לֻחוֹת הַבְּרִית, אֶחָד אֱלֹהֵינוּ שֶׁבַּשָּׁמַיִם וּבָאָרֶץ.

שְׁלֹשָׁה עָשָׂר מִי יוֹדֵעַ? שְׁלֹשָׁה עָשָׂר אֲנִי יוֹדֵעַ: שְׁלֹשָׁה עָשָׂר מִדַּיָּא. שְׁנֵים עָשָׂר שִׁבְטַיָּא, אַחַד עָשָׂר כּוֹכְבַיָּא, עֲשָׂרָה דִבְּרַיָּא, תִּשְׁעָה יַרְחֵי לֵדָה, שְׁמוֹנָה יְמֵי מִילָה, שִׁבְעָה יְמֵי שַׁבַּתָּא, שִׁשָּׁה סִדְרֵי מִשְׁנָה, חֲמִשָּׁה חֻמְשֵׁי תוֹרָה, אַרְבַּע אִמָּהוֹת, שְׁלֹשָׁה אָבוֹת, שְׁנֵי לֻחוֹת הַבְּרִית, אֶחָד אֱלֹהֵינוּ שֶׁבַּשָּׁמַיִם וּבָאָרֶץ.

נרצה

חֲמִשָּׁה מִי יוֹדֵעַ? חֲמִשָּׁה אֲנִי יוֹדֵעַ: חֲמִשָּׁה חֻמְשֵׁי תוֹרָה, אַרְבַּע אִמָּהוֹת, שְׁלֹשָׁה אָבוֹת, שְׁנֵי לֻחוֹת הַבְּרִית, אֶחָד אֱלֹהֵינוּ שֶׁבַּשָּׁמַיִם וּבָאָרֶץ.

שִׁשָּׁה מִי יוֹדֵעַ? שִׁשָּׁה אֲנִי יוֹדֵעַ: שִׁשָּׁה סִדְרֵי מִשְׁנָה, חֲמִשָּׁה חֻמְשֵׁי תוֹרָה, אַרְבַּע אִמָּהוֹת, שְׁלֹשָׁה אָבוֹת, שְׁנֵי לֻחוֹת הַבְּרִית, אֶחָד אֱלֹהֵינוּ שֶׁבַּשָּׁמַיִם וּבָאָרֶץ.

שִׁבְעָה מִי יוֹדֵעַ? שִׁבְעָה אֲנִי יוֹדֵעַ: שִׁבְעָה יְמֵי שַׁבַּתָּא, שִׁשָּׁה סִדְרֵי מִשְׁנָה, חֲמִשָּׁה חֻמְשֵׁי תוֹרָה, אַרְבַּע אִמָּהוֹת, שְׁלֹשָׁה אָבוֹת, שְׁנֵי לֻחוֹת הַבְּרִית, אֶחָד אֱלֹהֵינוּ שֶׁבַּשָּׁמַיִם וּבָאָרֶץ.

שְׁמוֹנָה מִי יוֹדֵעַ? שְׁמוֹנָה אֲנִי יוֹדֵעַ: שְׁמוֹנָה יְמֵי מִילָה, שִׁבְעָה יְמֵי שַׁבַּתָּא, שִׁשָּׁה סִדְרֵי מִשְׁנָה, חֲמִשָּׁה חֻמְשֵׁי תוֹרָה, אַרְבַּע אִמָּהוֹת, שְׁלֹשָׁה אָבוֹת, שְׁנֵי לֻחוֹת הַבְּרִית, אֶחָד אֱלֹהֵינוּ שֶׁבַּשָּׁמַיִם וּבָאָרֶץ.

תִּשְׁעָה מִי יוֹדֵעַ? תִּשְׁעָה אֲנִי יוֹדֵעַ: תִּשְׁעָה יַרְחֵי לֵדָה, שְׁמוֹנָה יְמֵי מִילָה, שִׁבְעָה יְמֵי שַׁבַּתָּא, שִׁשָּׁה סִדְרֵי מִשְׁנָה, חֲמִשָּׁה חֻמְשֵׁי תוֹרָה, אַרְבַּע אִמָּהוֹת, שְׁלֹשָׁה אָבוֹת, שְׁנֵי לֻחוֹת הַבְּרִית, אֶחָד אֱלֹהֵינוּ שֶׁבַּשָּׁמַיִם וּבָאָרֶץ.

עֲשָׂרָה מִי יוֹדֵעַ? עֲשָׂרָה אֲנִי יוֹדֵעַ: עֲשָׂרָה דִּבְּרַיָּא,

קָדוֹשׁ בִּמְלוּכָה, רַחוּם כַּהֲלָכָה שִׁנְאַנָּיו יֹאמְרוּ לוֹ:
לְךָ וּלְךָ, לְךָ כִּי לְךָ, לְךָ אַף לְךָ, לְךָ יהוה הַמַּמְלָכָה,
כִּי לוֹ נָאֶה, כִּי לוֹ יָאֶה.

תַּקִּיף בִּמְלוּכָה, תּוֹמֵךְ כַּהֲלָכָה תְּמִימָיו יֹאמְרוּ לוֹ:
לְךָ וּלְךָ, לְךָ כִּי לְךָ, לְךָ אַף לְךָ, לְךָ יהוה הַמַּמְלָכָה,
כִּי לוֹ נָאֶה, כִּי לוֹ יָאֶה.

The classic poem Adir Hu has been omitted because it is entirely a prayer for the restoration of the Temple.

אֶחָד מִי יוֹדֵעַ?

אֶחָד אֲנִי יוֹדֵעַ: אֶחָד אֱלֹהֵינוּ שֶׁבַּשָּׁמַיִם וּבָאָרֶץ.

שְׁנַיִם מִי יוֹדֵעַ? שְׁנַיִם אֲנִי יוֹדֵעַ: שְׁנֵי לֻחוֹת הַבְּרִית. אֶחָד אֱלֹהֵינוּ שֶׁבַּשָּׁמַיִם וּבָאָרֶץ.

שְׁלֹשָׁה מִי יוֹדֵעַ? שְׁלֹשָׁה אֲנִי יוֹדֵעַ: שְׁלֹשָׁה אָבוֹת, שְׁנֵי לֻחוֹת הַבְּרִית, אֶחָד אֱלֹהֵינוּ שֶׁבַּשָּׁמַיִם וּבָאָרֶץ.

אַרְבַּע מִי יוֹדֵעַ? אַרְבַּע אֲנִי יוֹדֵעַ: אַרְבַּע אִמָּהוֹת, שְׁלֹשָׁה אָבוֹת, שְׁנֵי לֻחוֹת הַבְּרִית, אֶחָד אֱלֹהֵינוּ שֶׁבַּשָּׁמַיִם וּבָאָרֶץ.

נרצה

כִּי לוֹ נָאֶה, כִּי לוֹ יָאֶה.

אַדִּיר בִּמְלוּכָה, בָּחוּר כַּהֲלָכָה, גְּדוּדָיו יֹאמְרוּ לוֹ:
לְךָ וּלְךָ, לְךָ כִּי לְךָ, לְךָ אַף לְךָ, לְךָ יהוה הַמַּמְלָכָה,
כִּי לוֹ נָאֶה, כִּי לוֹ יָאֶה.

דָּגוּל בִּמְלוּכָה, הָדוּר כַּהֲלָכָה, וָתִיקָיו יֹאמְרוּ לוֹ:
לְךָ וּלְךָ, לְךָ כִּי לְךָ, לְךָ אַף לְךָ, לְךָ יהוה הַמַּמְלָכָה,
כִּי לוֹ נָאֶה, כִּי לוֹ יָאֶה.

זַכַּאי בִּמְלוּכָה, חָסִין כַּהֲלָכָה טַפְסְרָיו יֹאמְרוּ לוֹ:
לְךָ וּלְךָ, לְךָ כִּי לְךָ, לְךָ אַף לְךָ, לְךָ יהוה הַמַּמְלָכָה,
כִּי לוֹ נָאֶה, כִּי לוֹ יָאֶה.

יָחִיד בִּמְלוּכָה, כַּבִּיר כַּהֲלָכָה לִמּוּדָיו יֹאמְרוּ לוֹ:
לְךָ וּלְךָ, לְךָ כִּי לְךָ, לְךָ אַף לְךָ, לְךָ יהוה הַמַּמְלָכָה,
כִּי לוֹ נָאֶה, כִּי לוֹ יָאֶה.

מוֹשֵׁל בִּמְלוּכָה, נוֹרָא כַּהֲלָכָה סְבִיבָיו יֹאמְרוּ לוֹ:
לְךָ וּלְךָ, לְךָ כִּי לְךָ, לְךָ אַף לְךָ, לְךָ יהוה הַמַּמְלָכָה,
כִּי לוֹ נָאֶה, כִּי לוֹ יָאֶה.

עָנָיו בִּמְלוּכָה, פּוֹדֶה כַּהֲלָכָה, צַדִּיקָיו יֹאמְרוּ לוֹ:
לְךָ וּלְךָ, לְךָ כִּי לְךָ, לְךָ אַף לְךָ, לְךָ יהוה הַמַּמְלָכָה,
כִּי לוֹ נָאֶה, כִּי לוֹ יָאֶה.

זוֹעֲמוּ סְדוֹמִים וְלוֹהֲטוּ בָּאֵשׁ בַּפֶּסַח,
חֻלַּץ לוֹט מֵהֶם וּמַצּוֹת אָפָה בְּקֵץ פֶּסַח,
טִאטֵאתָ אַדְמַת מוֹף וְנוֹף בְּעָבְרְךָ בַּפֶּסַח,
וַאֲמַרְתֶּם זֶבַח פֶּסַח.

יָהּ רֹאשׁ כָּל אוֹן מָחַצְתָּ בְּלֵיל שִׁמּוּר פֶּסַח,
כַּבִּיר, עַל בֵּן בְּכוֹר פָּסַחְתָּ בְּדַם פֶּסַח,
לְבִלְתִּי תֵּת מַשְׁחִית לָבֹא בִּפְתָחַי בַּפֶּסַח,
וַאֲמַרְתֶּם זֶבַח פֶּסַח.

מְסֻגֶּרֶת סֻגְּרָה בְּעִתּוֹתֵי פֶּסַח,
נִשְׁמְדָה מִדְיָן בִּצְלִיל שְׂעוֹרֵי עֹמֶר פֶּסַח,
שֹׂרְפוּ מִשְׁמַנֵּי פּוּל וְלוּד בִּיקַד יְקוֹד פֶּסַח,
וַאֲמַרְתֶּם זֶבַח פֶּסַח.

עוֹד הַיּוֹם בְּנֹב לַעֲמוֹד עַד גָּעָה עוֹנַת פֶּסַח,
פַּס יַד כָּתְבָה לְקַעֲקֵעַ צוּל בַּפֶּסַח,
צָפֹה הַצָּפִית עָרוֹךְ הַשֻּׁלְחָן בַּפֶּסַח,
וַאֲמַרְתֶּם זֶבַח פֶּסַח.

קָהָל כִּנְּסָה הֲדַסָּה לְשַׁלֵּשׁ צוֹם בַּפֶּסַח,
רֹאשׁ מִבֵּית רָשָׁע מָחַצְתָּ בְּעֵץ חֲמִשִּׁים בַּפֶּסַח,
שְׁתֵּי אֵלֶּה רֶגַע תָּבִיא לְעוּצִית בַּפֶּסַח,
תָּעֹז יָדְךָ וְתָרוּם יְמִינְךָ כְּלֵיל הִתְקַדֵּשׁ חַג פֶּסַח,
וַאֲמַרְתֶּם זֶבַח פֶּסַח.

נרצה

עוֹרַרְתָּ נִצְחֲךָ עָלָיו בְּנֶדֶד שְׁנַת לַיְלָה.
פּוּרָה תִדְרוֹךְ לְשׁוֹמֵר מַה מִּלַּיְלָה,
צָרַח כַּשּׁוֹמֵר וְשָׂח אָתָא בֹקֶר וְגַם לַיְלָה,
וַיְהִי בַּחֲצִי הַלַּיְלָה.

קָרֵב יוֹם אֲשֶׁר הוּא לֹא יוֹם וְלֹא לַיְלָה,
רָם הוֹדַע כִּי לְךָ הַיּוֹם אַף לְךָ הַלַּיְלָה,
שׁוֹמְרִים הַפְקֵד לְעִירְךָ כָּל הַיּוֹם וְכָל הַלַּיְלָה,
תָּאִיר כְּאוֹר יוֹם חֶשְׁכַת לַיְלָה,
וַיְהִי בַּחֲצִי הַלַּיְלָה.

וּבְכֵן וַאֲמַרְתֶּם זֶבַח פֶּסַח

אֹמֶץ גְּבוּרוֹתֶיךָ הִפְלֵאתָ בַּפֶּסַח,
בְּרֹאשׁ כָּל מוֹעֲדוֹת נִשֵּׂאתָ פֶּסַח,
גִּלִּיתָ לְאֶזְרָחִי חֲצוֹת לֵיל פֶּסַח,
וַאֲמַרְתֶּם זֶבַח פֶּסַח.

דְּלָתָיו דָּפַקְתָּ כְּחֹם הַיּוֹם בַּפֶּסַח,
הִסְעִיד נוֹצְצִים עֻגּוֹת מַצּוֹת בַּפֶּסַח,
וְאֶל הַבָּקָר רָץ זֵכֶר לְשׁוֹר עֵרֶךְ פֶּסַח,
וַאֲמַרְתֶּם זֶבַח פֶּסַח.

וּבְכֵן וַיְהִי בַּחֲצִי הַלַּיְלָה

אָז רוֹב נִסִּים הִפְלֵאתָ בַּלַּיְלָה,
בְּרֹאשׁ אַשְׁמוֹרֶת זֶה הַלַּיְלָה,
גֵּר צֶדֶק נִצַּחְתּוֹ כְּנֶחֱלַק לוֹ לַיְלָה,
וַיְהִי בַּחֲצִי הַלַּיְלָה.

דַּנְתָּ מֶלֶךְ גְּרָר בַּחֲלוֹם הַלַּיְלָה,
הִפְחַדְתָּ אֲרַמִּי בְּאֶמֶשׁ לַיְלָה,
וַיָּשַׂר יִשְׂרָאֵל לְמַלְאָךְ וַיּוּכַל לוֹ לַיְלָה,
וַיְהִי בַּחֲצִי הַלַּיְלָה.

זֶרַע בְּכוֹרֵי פַתְרוֹס מָחַצְתָּ בַּחֲצִי הַלַּיְלָה,
חֵילָם לֹא מָצְאוּ בְּקוּמָם בַּלַּיְלָה,
טִיסַת נְגִיד חֲרֹשֶׁת סִלִּיתָ בְּכוֹכְבֵי לַיְלָה,
וַיְהִי בַּחֲצִי הַלַּיְלָה.

יָעַץ מְחָרֵף לְנוֹפֵף אִוּוּי, הוֹבַשְׁתָּ פְּגָרָיו בַּלַּיְלָה,
כָּרַע בֵּל וּמַצָּבוֹ בְּאִישׁוֹן לַיְלָה,
לְאִישׁ חֲמוּדוֹת נִגְלָה רָז חֲזוֹת לַיְלָה,
וַיְהִי בַּחֲצִי הַלַּיְלָה.

מִשְׁתַּכֵּר בִּכְלֵי קֹדֶשׁ נֶהֱרַג בּוֹ בַּלַּיְלָה,
נוֹשַׁע מִבּוֹר אֲרָיוֹת פּוֹתֵר בְּעִתּוּתֵי לַיְלָה,
שִׂנְאָה נָטַר אֲגָגִי וְכָתַב סְפָרִים בַּלַּיְלָה,
וַיְהִי בַּחֲצִי הַלַּיְלָה.

נרצה

at God's behest, and why did it matter that his enemies had died? Was not Moses going to take Israel out of Egypt despite anyone who might stand in the way? Rashi explains that the men referred to were Dathan and Abiram, and they had just become impoverished, although they were still alive, the destitute being considered dead. That is, those who had previously tried to turn him in earlier were no longer a threat.

The answer to all of these questions seems to me to be this: Egypt's exile began because of the brothers' sins, the hatred they had for Joseph, whose explicit sin was bearing damaging reports to their father, what our sages called lashon hara, and everything devolved from there. Although eventually the brothers and their leader, Judah, confessed their sin when the Egyptian viceroy threatened to imprison them for espionage, they demonstrated their sincere repentance when they came to Benjamin's defense. However, we did not find that Joseph achieved atonement or removed his own sin somehow. When Moses contemplated his nation's subjugation, it became clear to him that there still were informers among them, and that that was why they were still being punished with bondage.

In Leviticus 26:40, it says that when the end of the exile is at hand, "They shall confess their sin and their fathers' sin, how they trespassed against Me, and also how they walked carelessly with Me."

Now, how can a living generation confess the long-gone fathers' sins? Why does the classic formula of confession include the statement, "But we and our ancestors have sinned?" The answer is that in order to annul the decree, it is not enough for us to abandon our evil ways, but rather we must verbally repudiate the sins that preceded them.

After "Joseph and all his brothers and that entire generation died," when Moses began to grasp the Israelites' situation and the injustice of bondage, the behavior of two particular Jews who were ready to betray him and inform on him proved to him that the Jewish people still clung to their ancestors' mistakes, and that is what led Pharaoh to seek to execute Moses, who fled to Midian. Then, when Moses first refused to go back to Egypt, he hinted that he believed that the Israelites deserved their lot, and God reminded him of this, as Rashi points out, by temporarily inflicting him with *tzaraat*, the typical punishment for speaking lashon hara.

Then, when Moses got on his way to Egypt, God notified him that the informers could no longer harm him. They were as good as dead, and Moses could not claim that the Israelites did not deserve to be redeemed! Thus, Moses's first confrontation with Pharaoh failed so that the Jewish taskmasters, who had the power to beat their brothers and inform on them to the Egyptians, would have a chance to prove that they would no longer physically coerce their brethren, they would not report on their doings to the Egyptian slave drivers, and they would not blame them for not filling the brick-quota. Instead, they pleaded with Moses and sought grace for a failure that they blamed only on themselves, and with heroic obedience they bore the burden of their tormentors' wrath. Only after all that could God tell Moses, "Now you will see what I will do to Pharaoh, for by a mighty hand will he set them free, and by a mighty hand will he drive them out of his land."

The Redemption comes about through Jewish unity: I have long felt that if Rashi had had enough time to prepare the complete edition of his commentary on the Torah, he would have noted that his comments on Exodus 2:14, are actually the plain meaning of the text, and not a midrashic interpretation. Moses rebuked a man for striking a fellow Hebrew, who responded: "Who made you a captain and a judge over us? Do you intend to kill me like you killed the Egyptian?" Moses was afraid, saying, "Indeed, the matter has become known." Rashi writes: Midrashically, Moses was saying, "I now know what I was wondering about before, [namely] how did Israel sin so that out of all seventy nations, [only] they are subject to back-breaking work? But now I see that they deserve it."

I make this claim because this idea, that Moses found a justification for his people's enslavement, can explain some puzzling details elsewhere in the parasha. Firstly, when God sent Moses to Pharaoh, he was to demand that he let His people go, and if not, then God would bring the plagues upon Pharaoh. However, when he first stood before Pharaoh, Pharaoh did not obey, and imposed even greater hardships upon the Israelites, decreeing that they would not even receive the raw materials they required to complete their quotas (ibid., 5:12):

So the people were scattered throughout the land of Egypt to gather stubble for straw. The taskmasters drove them, saying, 'finish your work each and every day, just like when there was straw.' The officers [the equivalent of kapos under the Nazi regime] of the children of Israel, whom Pharaoh's taskmasters had set over them, were beaten, saying, 'Why have you not fulfilled your brick-making quota both yesterday and today as you had done two days ago?' The officers of the children of Israel came and cried to Pharaoh, saying, 'Why would you do this to your servants? No straw is given to your servants, but they say to us, "make bricks!" and behold, your servants are beaten, but it is your people's fault.'

Why did this have to happen? Why would God test the Israelite officers, and why, after they also complained to Moses and blamed him for making their plight worse does God then repeat his promises to redeem the people?

"Now you will see what I will do to Pharaoh, for by a mighty hand will he set them free, and by a mighty hand will he drive them out of his land."

But before this new promise, Moses was not supposed to see Pharaoh drive them out? Why indeed did Moses go before Pharaoh if he was doomed to fail? It would have made more sense for Moses's initial encounter with Pharaoh to unfold as it did in Exodus 7, when he and Aaron went again before Pharaoh and turned the staff into a serpent, and which immediately preceded the succession of plagues.

Secondly, what is the meaning of this verse that appears after Moses accepted his historic mission after a long series of refusals, and only after he informed Jethro that he was leaving Midian to return to Egypt (4:19)?

"The Lord said to Moses in Midian: 'Go, return to Egypt, for all the men who sought your life have died.'"

Why did God need to tell Moses to go back to Egypt if he was already on his way

He has comforted all her ruins;
He has made her wilderness like Eden,
and her desert plain like the Lord's garden.
Gladness and happiness shall be found within her,
thanksgiving, and the sound of music.
I will greatly rejoice in the Lord,
my soul will exult in my God,
for He clothed me with the raiment of salvation;
He would enwrap me with a coat of vindication,
like a groom donning distinction,
and as a bride applies her ornaments.
I will recount the Lord's kindnesses,
the Lord's praises,
according to all that the Lord did for us;
and the great goodness toward the house of Israel,
which He did for them
according to His compassion and great mercy.
He said, "they are My people, after all;
children who will not lie;"
and He was a Savior to them.
Throughout their affliction,
He was afflicted,
and His personal angel saved them;
in His love and in His pity He redeemed them;
He always bore them and carried them
in the days of old.

Nirtza

נִחַם כָּל חָרְבֹתֶיהָ
וַיָּשֶׂם מִדְבָּרָהּ כְּעֵדֶן
וְעַרְבָתָהּ כְּגַן יהוה;
שָׂשׂוֹן וְשִׂמְחָה יִמָּצֵא בָהּ
תּוֹדָה וְקוֹל זִמְרָה.
שׂוֹשׂ אָשִׂישׂ בַּיהוה
תָּגֵל נַפְשִׁי בֵּאלֹהַי
כִּי הִלְבִּישַׁנִי בִּגְדֵי יֶשַׁע
מְעִיל צְדָקָה יְעָטָנִי;
כֶּחָתָן יְכַהֵן פְּאֵר
וְכַכַּלָּה תַּעְדֶּה כֵלֶיהָ.
חַסְדֵי יהוה אַזְכִּיר תְּהִלֹּת יהוה
כְּעַל, כֹּל אֲשֶׁר גְּמָלָנוּ יהוה;
וְרַב טוּב לְבֵית יִשְׂרָאֵל
אֲשֶׁר גְּמָלָם כְּרַחֲמָיו וּכְרֹב חֲסָדָיו.
וַיֹּאמֶר אַךְ עַמִּי הֵמָּה
בָּנִים לֹא יְשַׁקֵּרוּ;
וַיְהִי לָהֶם לְמוֹשִׁיעַ.
בְּכָל צָרָתָם לוֹ צָר
וּמַלְאַךְ פָּנָיו הוֹשִׁיעָם
בְּאַהֲבָתוֹ וּבְחֶמְלָתוֹ הוּא גְאָלָם;
וַיְנַטְּלֵם וַיְנַשְּׂאֵם כָּל יְמֵי עוֹלָם.

נרצה

and I will not be afraid;
for Yah, the LORD, is my strength and song,
and He became my salvation.
You shall draw water in celebration
from the wells of salvation.
And on that day you will say
Thank the Lord, call His name,
Make His doings known among the nations;
Make mention, for His name is exalted.
Make music unto the Lord,
for He has given us pride;
this is made known throughout the earth.
Revel and sing joyously, inhabitant of Zion,
for the Holy One of Israel is great in your midst.

How beautiful are the herald's feet
upon the mountains
Proclaimer of peace,
the herald of good tidings,
Proclaimer of salvation;
Who says to Zion, "your God reigns!"
Break out and sing joyously with each other,
O ruins of Jerusalem,
for the Lord has comforted His people;
He has redeemed Jerusalem.
The Lord has bared His holy arm
in the eyes of all the nations,
And everyone on earth saw our God's salvation.

Nirtza For the Lord has comforted Zion;

וְלֹא אֶפְחָד;
כִּי עָזִּי וְזִמְרָת יָהּ יהוה
וַיְהִי לִי לִישׁוּעָה.
וּשְׁאַבְתֶּם מַיִם בְּשָׂשׂוֹן
מִמַּעַיְנֵי הַיְשׁוּעָה.
וַאֲמַרְתֶּם בַּיּוֹם הַהוּא
הוֹדוּ לַיהוה קִרְאוּ בִשְׁמוֹ
הוֹדִיעוּ בָעַמִּים עֲלִילֹתָיו;
הַזְכִּירוּ כִּי נִשְׂגָּב שְׁמוֹ.
זַמְּרוּ יהוה כִּי גֵאוּת עָשָׂה;
מוּדַעַת זֹאת, בְּכָל הָאָרֶץ.
צַהֲלִי וָרֹנִּי יוֹשֶׁבֶת צִיּוֹן
כִּי גָדוֹל בְּקִרְבֵּךְ קְדוֹשׁ יִשְׂרָאֵל.

מַה נָּאווּ עַל הֶהָרִים רַגְלֵי מְבַשֵּׂר
מַשְׁמִיעַ שָׁלוֹם מְבַשֵּׂר טוֹב
מַשְׁמִיעַ יְשׁוּעָה;
אֹמֵר לְצִיּוֹן מָלַךְ אֱלֹהָיִךְ.
פִּצְחוּ רַנְּנוּ יַחְדָּו חָרְבוֹת יְרוּשָׁלָ͏ִם
כִּי נִחַם יהוה עַמּוֹ, גָּאַל יְרוּשָׁלָ͏ִם.
חָשַׂף יהוה אֶת זְרוֹעַ קָדְשׁוֹ לְעֵינֵי כָּל הַגּוֹיִם
וְרָאוּ כָּל אַפְסֵי אָרֶץ אֵת יְשׁוּעַת אֱלֹהֵינוּ.

נרצה כִּי נִחַם יהוה צִיּוֹן

With trumpets and the sound of the horn
    make noise before the King, the Lord.
Let the sea and its fullness thunder;
    Earth, and all who dwell thereon;
Let the rivers clap their hands;
    the mountains will sing for joy as one.
Before the Lord, for He has come   to judge the earth;
He will judge the world with justice
    and the nations with fairness.

Some sing the following psalm before Birkat Hamazon, although this is not mentioned in the codes. In any event, it is appropriate for this part of the seder.

A Song of Ascents.
When the Lord brought back the returnees of Zion
    we were like dreamers.
Then our mouth became filled with laughter
    and our tongue with joyous song;
Then they said among the nations
    "The Lord did great things with these."
The Lord did great things with us;   we were gladdened.
Bring back our returnees, O Lord,
    like the streams in the Negev.
Those who sow in tears   shall reap in joy.
He may go on his way crying   carrying the sack of seeds;
He shall come on his way joyously   carrying his sheaves.

The Prophet Isaiah's Song of Redemption:

You shall say on that day:
I will thank You, O Lord,
for although You were angry at me,
Your anger would turn away,
and You would comfort me.
Behold, God is my salvation;
I will trust,

בַּחֲצֹצְרוֹת וְקוֹל שׁוֹפָר	הָרִיעוּ לִפְנֵי הַמֶּלֶךְ יהוה.
יִרְעַם הַיָּם וּמְלֹאוֹ	תֵּבֵל וְיֹשְׁבֵי בָהּ.
נְהָרוֹת יִמְחֲאוּ כָף	יַחַד הָרִים יְרַנֵּנוּ.
לִפְנֵי יהוה כִּי בָא	לִשְׁפֹּט הָאָרֶץ;
יִשְׁפֹּט תֵּבֵל בְּצֶדֶק	וְעַמִּים בְּמֵישָׁרִים.

יש נוהגין לשיר פרק זה לפני ברכת המזון, ואיננו מוזכר בפוסקים, וראוי לשוררו כאן:

שִׁיר הַמַּעֲלוֹת;

בְּשׁוּב יהוה אֶת שִׁיבַת צִיּוֹן	הָיִינוּ כְּחֹלְמִים.
אָז יִמָּלֵא שְׂחוֹק פִּינוּ	וּלְשׁוֹנֵנוּ רִנָּה;
אָז יֹאמְרוּ בַגּוֹיִם	הִגְדִּיל יהוה לַעֲשׂוֹת עִם אֵלֶּה.
הִגְדִּיל יהוה לַעֲשׂוֹת עִמָּנוּ	הָיִינוּ שְׂמֵחִים.
שׁוּבָה יהוה אֶת שְׁבִיתֵנוּ	כַּאֲפִיקִים בַּנֶּגֶב.
הַזֹּרְעִים בְּדִמְעָה	בְּרִנָּה יִקְצֹרוּ.
הָלוֹךְ יֵלֵךְ וּבָכֹה	נֹשֵׂא מֶשֶׁךְ הַזָּרַע;
בֹּא יָבֹא בְרִנָּה	נֹשֵׂא אֲלֻמֹּתָיו.

שירת הגאולה לישעיהו הנביא זכור לטוב:

וְאָמַרְתָּ בַּיּוֹם הַהוּא

אוֹדְךָ יהוה כִּי אָנַפְתָּ בִּי;

יָשֹׁב אַפְּךָ וּתְנַחֲמֵנִי.

הִנֵּה אֵל יְשׁוּעָתִי, אֶבְטַח

נרצה

For His anger is but a moment;   His grace is for life;
He may retire for the evening in crying,
                                   but in joy by morning.
When I was comfortable I had said
                                   I shall not be budged.
O Lord, amidst Your grace
                                   You set my mountain as a stronghold;
[When] You hid Your countenance   I was panicked.
To You, O Lord, would I call
                                   and to the Lord would I supplicate.
What benefit is there from [spilling] my blood
                                   were I to descend to the wastes?
Shall dust thank You?   Will it relate Your truth?
Hear, O Lord, and favor me;   Lord, be a Helper for me.
You turned my grieving   into dancing for me;
You loosened my sackcloth
                                   and girded me with happiness;
So that glory may sing to You, and not be silent;
                O Lord, my God, I will thank You forever.

See Rosh Hashana 30b, which discusses the rebuilding of the Temple and the reinstitution of the sacrificial service as taking place on Passover, and this is the psalm intended for that event:

A Psalm.
Sing a new song to the Lord for He has done amazing things;
    His right hand and His holy arm have saved for Him.
The Lord made His salvation known;
    He revealed His righteousness to the eyes of the nations.
He remembered His mercy and faithfulness
                                   for the house of Israel;
Everyone on earth saw   our God's salvation.
Let the entire land shout to the Lord;
                break out, sing for joy, and make music.
Make music to the Lord with the harp
                with the harp and a melodic voice.

כִּי רֶגַע בְּאַפּוֹ	חַיִּים בִּרְצוֹנוֹ;
בָּעֶרֶב, יָלִין בֶּכִי	וְלַבֹּקֶר רִנָּה.
וַאֲנִי אָמַרְתִּי בְשַׁלְוִי	בַּל אֶמּוֹט לְעוֹלָם.
יהוה בִּרְצוֹנְךָ	הֶעֱמַדְתָּה לְהַרְרִי עֹז;
הִסְתַּרְתָּ פָנֶיךָ	הָיִיתִי נִבְהָל.
אֵלֶיךָ יְהוָה אֶקְרָא	וְאֶל אֲדֹנָי אֶתְחַנָּן.
מַה בֶּצַע בְּדָמִי	בְּרִדְתִּי אֶל שָׁחַת;
הֲיוֹדְךָ עָפָר	הֲיַגִּיד אֲמִתֶּךָ.
שְׁמַע יְהוָה וְחָנֵּנִי	יהוה הֱיֵה עֹזֵר לִי.
הָפַכְתָּ מִסְפְּדִי	לְמָחוֹל לִי;
פִּתַּחְתָּ שַׂקִּי	וַתְּאַזְּרֵנִי שִׂמְחָה.
לְמַעַן יְזַמֶּרְךָ כָבוֹד וְלֹא יִדֹּם	
יְהוָה אֱלֹהַי לְעוֹלָם אוֹדֶךָּ.	

הערה: ראה ראש השנה ל' ע"א ששם מדובר בסיום בנין בית המקדש וחידוש העבודה בפסח, ושיר זה מיועד לחנוכת הבית.

מִזְמוֹר

שִׁירוּ לַיהוָה שִׁיר חָדָשׁ, כִּי נִפְלָאוֹת עָשָׂה

הוֹשִׁיעָה לּוֹ יְמִינוֹ וּזְרוֹעַ קָדְשׁוֹ.

הוֹדִיעַ יְהוָה יְשׁוּעָתוֹ	לְעֵינֵי הַגּוֹיִם גִּלָּה צִדְקָתוֹ.
זָכַר חַסְדּוֹ וֶאֱמוּנָתוֹ	לְבֵית יִשְׂרָאֵל;
רָאוּ כָל אַפְסֵי אָרֶץ	אֵת יְשׁוּעַת אֱלֹהֵינוּ.
הָרִיעוּ לַיהוָה כָּל הָאָרֶץ	פִּצְחוּ וְרַנְּנוּ וְזַמֵּרוּ.
זַמְּרוּ לַיהוָה בְּכִנּוֹר	בְּכִנּוֹר וְקוֹל זִמְרָה.

Nirtza

It is customary to complete the seder with a series of songs and poems of praise, but "the more one recounts the story of the exodus from Egypt, the better."

**The Passover seder has been completed according to its law,
according to all its matters and statutes.
Just as we have merited to perform it,
so may we merit to perform it [again].
O Pure One Who dwells in the habitation,
Who chooses the innumerable communal congregation,
the plantings of the sapling,
through the songs of Hallel,
stand redeemed joyfully in Zion.**

The original version of this piyut as found in the exilic Yotzer for Shabbat Hagadol is:

The Passover seder has been completed according to its law, according to all its matters and statutes. Just as we have merited to arrange it, so may we merit to perform it. O Pure One Who dwells in the habitation, raise up the innumerable communal congregation. May You soon guide the plantings of the sapling to be redeemed joyfully in Zion.

The text has been thankfully updated to reflect the new reality, although the Hebrew rhyme and meter have been preserved.

Songs of praise and thanksgiving for the fulfillment of the prophecies of redemption:

**A Psalm; a Song of the Dedication of the Temple by David.
I will extol You, O Lord, for You have drawn me up
    and You did not let my enemies rejoice over me.
O Lord, my God   I cried to You and You healed me.
O Lord, You raised my soul from the nether-world;
    You kept me alive, so I would not go down to the pit.
Make music to the Lord, O His pious ones
    and thank His holy memory.**

נִרְצָה

נוהגים לשיר סדרת פיוטי שבח והודיה לה' יתברך. וכל המרבה לספר ביציאת מצרים, הרי זה משובח.

חֲסַל סִדּוּר פֶּסַח כְּהִלְכָתוֹ
כְּכָל מִשְׁפָּטוֹ וְחֻקָּתוֹ.
כַּאֲשֶׁר זָכִינוּ לַעֲשׂוֹת אוֹתוֹ
כֵּן נִזְכֶּה לַעֲשׂוֹתוֹ.
זָךְ שׁוֹכֵן מְעוֹנָה
בּוֹחֵר קְהַל עֲדַת מִי מָנָה.
בְּשִׁירֵי הַלֵּל נִטְעֵי כַנָּה
פְּדוּיִם בְּצִיּוֹן בְּרִנָּה.

הערה: הנוסח המקורי על פי היוצר לשבת הגדול הוא:
חֲסַל סִדּוּר פֶּסַח כְּהִלְכָתוֹ, כְּכָל מִשְׁפָּטוֹ וְחֻקָּתוֹ.
כַּאֲשֶׁר זָכִינוּ לְסַדֵּר אוֹתוֹ כֵּן נִזְכֶּה לַעֲשׂוֹתוֹ.
זָךְ שׁוֹכֵן מְעוֹנָה קוֹמֵם קְהַל עֲדַת מִי מָנָה.
בְּקָרוֹב נַהֵל נִטְעֵי כַנָּה, פְּדוּיִם לְצִיּוֹן בְּרִנָּה.
והנוסח כאן תוקן באותו המקצב בשביל המציאות המחודשת ב"ה.

מזמורי שבח והודיה על התקיימות נבואות הגאולה:

מִזְמוֹר, שִׁיר חֲנֻכַּת הַבַּיִת לְדָוִד.
אֲרוֹמִמְךָ יהוה כִּי דִלִּיתָנִי   וְלֹא שִׂמַּחְתָּ אֹיְבַי לִי.
יהוה אֱלֹהָי   שִׁוַּעְתִּי אֵלֶיךָ, וַתִּרְפָּאֵנִי.
יהוה הֶעֱלִיתָ מִן שְׁאוֹל נַפְשִׁי   חִיִּיתַנִי מִיָּרְדִי בוֹר.
זַמְּרוּ לַיהוה חֲסִידָיו   וְהוֹדוּ לְזֵכֶר קָדְשׁוֹ.

The "Three-Faceted" Blessing

**Blessed are You, O Lord, our God,
King of the universe,
for the vine and for the fruit of the vine,
for the yield of the field,
and for the enviable, goodly, and expansive land,
which You wanted and gave to us and our fathers,
so we might eat from its fruit
and be satisfied from its goodness.**

Uphold for us, O Lord our God,
Your people Israel,
Your city Jerusalem,
Your glorious abode, Zion,
and Your altar and Your temple,
and we shall bless You in holiness and in purity.

[On Shabbat: **Be pleased with us and strengthen us on this Sabbath day, and**]

**gladden us on this day of the Festival of Matzot,
for You, O Lord, are good
and do good for all,
and we thank You
for the land and for the fruit of the vine.
Blessed are You, O Lord,
for the land and for the fruit of the vine.**

Nothing is eaten after the Korban Pesah for the rest of the night, but one may still drink water.

ברכה מעין שלש

בָּרוּךְ אַתָּה יהוה אֱלֹהֵינוּ מֶלֶךְ הָעוֹלָם
עַל הַגֶּפֶן וְעַל פְּרִי הַגֶּפֶן
וְעַל תְּנוּבַת הַשָּׂדֶה
וְעַל אֶרֶץ חֶמְדָּה טוֹבָה וּרְחָבָה
שֶׁרָצִיתָ וְהִנְחַלְתָּ לָנוּ וְלַאֲבוֹתֵינוּ
לֶאֱכֹל מִפִּרְיָהּ וְלִשְׂבֹּעַ מִטּוּבָהּ.
קַיֵּם לָנוּ יהוה אֱלֹהֵינוּ
אֶת יִשְׂרָאֵל עַמֶּךָ
וְאֶת יְרוּשָׁלַיִם עִירֶךָ
וְאֶת צִיּוֹן מִשְׁכַּן כְּבוֹדֶךָ
וְאֶת מִזְבְּחֶךָ וְאֶת הֵיכָלֶךָ.
וּנְבָרֶכְךָ בִּקְדֻשָּׁה וּבְטָהֳרָה

[בשבת: וּרְצֵה וְהַחֲלִיצֵנוּ בְּיוֹם הַשַּׁבָּת הַזֶּה]

וְשַׂמְּחֵנוּ בְּיוֹם חַג הַמַּצּוֹת הַזֶּה
כִּי אַתָּה יהוה טוֹב וּמֵטִיב לַכֹּל
וְנוֹדֶה לְּךָ עַל הָאָרֶץ וְעַל פְּרִי הַגֶּפֶן.
בָּרוּךְ אַתָּה יהוה, עַל הָאָרֶץ וְעַל פְּרִי הַגֶּפֶן.

ברכת השיר

ואין מפטירים אחר הפסח אפיקומן,
שאינו טועם אחר כך כלום כל הלילה, חוץ מן המים.

Your name, shall be praised forever, our King,
God, the great and holy King
in the heavens and in the earth.
For it is pleasant for You,
O Lord our God and God of our fathers,
song, lauding, praise, hymn,
boldness, dominion, eternity, greatness, might
psalm, splendor, holiness, kingship,
blessings and thanks, from now and forever.
Blessed are You O Lord, God,
the greatly praised King,
God of thanks,
Master of wonders,
Chooser of the musical songs
King, God, the Life of all worlds.

Some omit the following blessing:

Blessed are You, O Lord, our God, King of the universe, Creator of the fruit of the vine.

The fourth cup is then drunk. As mentioned above, it is recommended to pour a fifth cup of wine to be drunk after reciting the Great Hallel. The following "three-faceted" blessing is recited once one has finished all of the cups of wine that he intended to drink:

Birkat Hashir

יִשְׁתַּבַּח שִׁמְךָ לָעַד מַלְכֵּנוּ
הָאֵל הַמֶּלֶךְ הַגָּדוֹל וְהַקָּדוֹשׁ
בַּשָּׁמַיִם וּבָאָרֶץ
כִּי לְךָ נָאֶה, יהוה אֱלֹהֵינוּ וֵאלֹהֵי אֲבוֹתֵינוּ
שִׁיר וּשְׁבָחָה, הַלֵּל וְזִמְרָה
עֹז וּמֶמְשָׁלָה, נֶצַח גְּדֻלָּה וּגְבוּרָה
תְּהִלָּה וְתִפְאֶרֶת, קְדֻשָּׁה וּמַלְכוּת
בְּרָכוֹת וְהוֹדָאוֹת מֵעַתָּה וְעַד עוֹלָם.
בָּרוּךְ אַתָּה יהוה, אֵל מֶלֶךְ גָּדוֹל בַּתִּשְׁבָּחוֹת
אֵל הַהוֹדָאוֹת, אֲדוֹן הַנִּפְלָאוֹת
הַבּוֹחֵר בְּשִׁירֵי זִמְרָה
מֶלֶךְ אֵל, חֵי הָעוֹלָמִים.

מנהג האשכנזים לברך ברכה זו, ומנהג הבית יוסף שאין לברך:

בָּרוּךְ אַתָּה יהוה, אֱלֹהֵינוּ מֶלֶךְ הָעוֹלָם
בּוֹרֵא פְּרִי הַגָּפֶן.

ושותים את הכוס הרביעי. יש למזוג כוס חמישי ולומר עליו ההלל הגדול, כדלעיל. ואחרי שתיית הכוס האחרון, יברך הברכה מעין שלש.

ברכת השיר

The King sitting on a lofty and elevated throne.
He dwells forever;
His name is lofty and holy.
And as it is written,
"Sing, You righteous, to the Lord;
Praise is beautiful from the upright."
You shall be praised by the mouth of the upright,
You will be blessed by the words of the righteous,
You will be elevated by the tongues of the devout,
and You will be sanctified in the midst of holy ones.

And in the assemblies of the myriads
of Your people, the House of Israel,
in joyous song Your name will be glorified,
our King, in every generation
as it is the obligation of all creatures before You,
O Lord our God and the God of our fathers,
to thank, to praise, to laud,
to glorify, to exalt, to lavish,
to bless, to elevate, and to extol beyond every word
of Your anointed servant David
the son of Jesse's songs and praises.

Birkat Hashir

הַמֶּלֶךְ הַיּוֹשֵׁב עַל כִּסֵּא רָם וְנִשָּׂא.
שׁוֹכֵן עַד
מָרוֹם וְקָדוֹשׁ שְׁמוֹ.
וְכָתוּב: רַנְּנוּ צַדִּיקִים בַּיהוה
לַיְשָׁרִים נָאוָה תְהִלָּה.
בְּפִי יְשָׁרִים תִּתְהַלָּל
וּבְדִבְרֵי צַדִּיקִים תִּתְבָּרַךְ
וּבִלְשׁוֹן חֲסִידִים תִּתְרוֹמָם
וּבְקֶרֶב קְדוֹשִׁים תִּתְקַדָּשׁ.

וּבְמַקְהֲלוֹת רִבְבוֹת עַמְּךָ בֵּית יִשְׂרָאֵל
בְּרִנָּה יִתְפָּאֵר שִׁמְךָ, מַלְכֵּנוּ, בְּכָל דּוֹר וָדוֹר
שֶׁכֵּן חוֹבַת כָּל הַיְצוּרִים לְפָנֶיךָ
יהוה אֱלֹהֵינוּ וֵאלֹהֵי אֲבוֹתֵינוּ
לְהוֹדוֹת לְהַלֵּל לְשַׁבֵּחַ
לְפָאֵר לְרוֹמֵם לְהַדֵּר
לְבָרֵךְ לְעַלֵּה וּלְקַלֵּס
עַל כָּל דִּבְרֵי שִׁירוֹת וְתִשְׁבְּחוֹת דָּוִד בֶּן יִשַׁי,
עַבְדְּךָ מְשִׁיחֶךָ.

ברכת השיר

glorify, exalt, extol, sanctify,
and ascribe kingship to Your name, our King.
For every mouth shall thank You,
every tongue shall swear by You,
every knee shall bow to You,
all that stand tall shall prostrate before You,
all hearts shall fear You,
and all innards and counsels
shall make music to Your name,
as per what is said,
All of my bones shall say,
"Lord, who is like You?"
He rescues the pauper from one who is stronger,
and the pauper and the destitute from his robber.
Who is like You,
and who is comparable to You,
and who can match You?
The great, strong, and awesome God,
the Supreme God,
Acquirer of heaven and earth.
We shall praise, extol, and glorify You,
and we will bless Your holy Name,
as it is said
Of David. Bless the Lord, O my soul,
and all of my innards, His holy Name.

Birkat Hashir

The God, in Your bold power
The Great, in Your glorious name
The Mighty One for eternity Supremely Awesome

וִיפָאֲרוּ וִירוֹמְמוּ וְיַעֲרִיצוּ וְיַקְדִישׁוּ
וְיַמְלִיכוּ אֶת שִׁמְךָ מַלְכֵּנוּ.
כִּי כָל פֶּה לְךָ יוֹדֶה
וְכָל לָשׁוֹן לְךָ תִשָּׁבַע
וְכָל בֶּרֶךְ לְךָ תִכְרַע
וְכָל קוֹמָה לְפָנֶיךָ תִשְׁתַּחֲוֶה
וְכָל לְבָבוֹת יִירָאוּךָ
וְכָל קֶרֶב וּכְלָיוֹת יְזַמְּרוּ לִשְׁמֶךָ
כַּדָּבָר שֶׁנֶּאֱמַר, כָּל עַצְמֹתַי תֹּאמַרְנָה
יהוה מִי כָמוֹךָ.
מַצִּיל עָנִי מֵחָזָק מִמֶּנּוּ
וְעָנִי וְאֶבְיוֹן מִגֹּזְלוֹ.
מִי יִדְמֶה לָּךְ   וּמִי יִשְׁוֶה לָּךְ   וּמִי יַעֲרָךְ לָךְ?
הָאֵל, הַגָּדוֹל, הַגִּבּוֹר, וְהַנּוֹרָא
אֵל עֶלְיוֹן, קֹנֵה שָׁמַיִם וָאָרֶץ.
נְהַלֶּלְךָ וּנְשַׁבֵּחֲךָ וּנְפָאֶרְךָ
וּנְבָרֵךְ אֶת שֵׁם קָדְשֶׁךָ, כָּאָמוּר:
לְדָוִד, בָּרְכִי נַפְשִׁי אֶת יהוה
וְכָל קְרָבַי אֶת שֵׁם קָדְשׁוֹ.

ברכת השיר

הָאֵל בְּתַעֲצֻמוֹת עֻזֶּךָ
הַגָּדוֹל בִּכְבוֹד שְׁמֶךָ
הַגִּבּוֹר לָנֶצַח וְהַנּוֹרָא בְּנוֹרְאוֹתֶיךָ

and our tongue with noise as its many waves,
our lips with praise as the expanses of the sky,
our eyes as bright as the sun and the moon
our hands as outspread as the vultures of the sky,
and our feet as swift as gazelles,
we could not sufficiently thank You
O Lord, our God and the God of our fathers,
or bless Your Name for one thousandth
of the millions and billions of times
that You have done favors for our ancestors and us.
You, O Lord, our God, delivered us from Egypt
and You redeemed us from the house of bondage.
During famine, You fed us,
and during plenty You provided for us.
You rescued us from the sword,
You spared us from pestilence,
and You saved us
from horrific and persistent diseases.
Your mercy has helped us until now,
and Your kindness has not abandoned us,
and You will never forsake us, O Lord our God.
Therefore, the limbs that You set within us,
the spirits and souls
that You breathed into our noses,
and the tongues that You placed in our mouths,
all of them will thank, bless, praise,

Birkat Hashir

וּלְשׁוֹנֵנוּ רִנָּה כַּהֲמוֹן גַּלָּיו
וְשִׂפְתוֹתֵינוּ שֶׁבַח כְּמֶרְחֲבֵי רָקִיעַ
וְעֵינֵינוּ מְאִירוֹת כַּשֶּׁמֶשׁ וְכַיָּרֵחַ
וְיָדֵינוּ פְרוּשׂוֹת כְּנִשְׁרֵי שָׁמַיִם
וְרַגְלֵינוּ קַלּוֹת כָּאַיָּלוֹת
אֵין אֲנַחְנוּ מַסְפִּיקִים לְהוֹדוֹת לְךָ
יהוה אֱלֹהֵינוּ וֵאלֹהֵי אֲבוֹתֵינוּ
וּלְבָרֵךְ אֶת שְׁמֶךָ עַל אַחַת מֵאֶלֶף אַלְפֵי אֲלָפִים
וְרִבֵּי רְבָבוֹת פְּעָמִים
הַטּוֹבוֹת שֶׁעָשִׂיתָ עִם אֲבוֹתֵינוּ וְעִמָּנוּ.
מִמִּצְרַיִם גְּאַלְתָּנוּ, יהוה אֱלֹהֵינוּ
וּמִבֵּית עֲבָדִים פְּדִיתָנוּ
בְּרָעָב זַנְתָּנוּ וּבְשָׂבָע כִּלְכַּלְתָּנוּ
מֵחֶרֶב הִצַּלְתָּנוּ וּמִדֶּבֶר מִלַּטְתָּנוּ
וּמֵחֳלָאִים רָעִים וְנֶאֱמָנִים דִּלִּיתָנוּ.
עַד הֵנָּה עֲזָרוּנוּ רַחֲמֶיךָ
וְלֹא עֲזָבוּנוּ חֲסָדֶיךָ
וְאַל תִּטְּשֵׁנוּ, יהוה אֱלֹהֵינוּ, לָנֶצַח.
עַל כֵּן אֵבָרִים שֶׁפִּלַּגְתָּ בָּנוּ
וְרוּחַ וּנְשָׁמָה שֶׁנָּפַחְתָּ בְּאַפֵּינוּ
וְלָשׁוֹן אֲשֶׁר שַׂמְתָּ בְּפִינוּ
הֵן הֵם יוֹדוּ וִיבָרְכוּ וִישַׁבְּחוּ

and it is befitting to make music to Your name
and You are God forever and ever.

As mentioned above, some believe that Birkat Hashir is only Nishmat, and therefore they begin here:

Birkat Hashir

The souls of all living things
shall bless Your Name, O Lord our God,
and the spirits of all flesh shall constantly glorify
and exalt Your memory, our King.
From the beginning of time until all time,
You are God,
and besides You we have no king, deliverer, savior,
redeemer, rescuer, provider, or caretaker
in any time of trouble or distress.
We have no king but You!
The God of the early generations
and the latter generations,
God of all creatures,
Master of all procreators,
Who is lauded through the multitude of praises,
Who guides His world with kindness
and His creatures with mercy.
The Lord neither sleeps nor slumbers.
It is He Who rouses the slumberers
and awakens the sleepers
and allows the mute to speak, releases the restrained,
supports the falling, and straightens the bent.
We thank only You.
If our mouths were as full of song as the sea,

וּלְשִׁמְךָ נָאֶה לְזַמֵּר
וּמֵעוֹלָם וְעַד עוֹלָם אַתָּה אֵל.

ויש נוהגים להתחיל ברכת השיר כאן:

נִשְׁמַת כָּל חַי תְּבָרֵךְ אֶת שִׁמְךָ, יְהֹוָה אֱלֹהֵינוּ
וְרוּחַ כָּל בָּשָׂר תְּפָאֵר וּתְרוֹמֵם זִכְרְךָ, מַלְכֵּנוּ, תָּמִיד.
מִן הָעוֹלָם וְעַד הָעוֹלָם אַתָּה אֵל
וּמִבַּלְעָדֶיךָ אֵין לָנוּ מֶלֶךְ גּוֹאֵל וּמוֹשִׁיעַ
פּוֹדֶה וּמַצִּיל וּמְפַרְנֵס וּמְרַחֵם
בְּכָל עֵת צָרָה וְצוּקָה.
אֵין לָנוּ מֶלֶךְ אֶלָּא אַתָּה.
אֱלֹהֵי הָרִאשׁוֹנִים וְהָאַחֲרוֹנִים
אֱלוֹהַּ כָּל בְּרִיּוֹת
אֲדוֹן כָּל תּוֹלָדוֹת,
הַמְהֻלָּל בְּרֹב הַתִּשְׁבָּחוֹת
הַמְנַהֵג עוֹלָמוֹ בְּחֶסֶד
וּבְרִיּוֹתָיו בְּרַחֲמִים.
וַיהֹוָה לֹא יָנוּם וְלֹא יִישָׁן.
הַמְעוֹרֵר יְשֵׁנִים וְהַמֵּקִיץ נִרְדָּמִים
וְהַמֵּשִׂיחַ אִלְּמִים וְהַמַּתִּיר אֲסוּרִים
וְהַסּוֹמֵךְ נוֹפְלִים וְהַזּוֹקֵף כְּפוּפִים.
לְךָ לְבַדְּךָ אֲנַחְנוּ מוֹדִים.
אִלּוּ פִינוּ מָלֵא שִׁירָה כַּיָּם

ברכת השיר

Birkat Hashir

The medieval authorities disagree regarding what exactly Birkat Hashir is. Maimonides's view is that of Rabbi Judah's in the Talmud, that Birkat Hashir is the blessing known as *Y'hal'lucha*:

All of Your works shall praise You, Lord our God,
and Your pious and righteous ones who do Your will
and all of Your people, the House of Israel,
will thank Your name in commotion
For You, O Lord
are good to thank
and it is pleasant to make music for Your name
and You are God forever and ever.
Blessed are You, O Lord, the King
Who is praised and flattered,
living and enduring,
Who will always reign forever and everlasting.

The blessing on the wine is then recited, and the wine is then drunk.

According to Rabbi Johanan, Birkat Hashir is the prayer known as Nishmat. Others believe that Birkat Hashir is a combination of Y'hal'lucha and Nishmat, and there is then disagreement regarding the order. According to the standard Ashkenazic rite, Y'hal'lucha is said first, but its concluding blessing is omitted:

All of Your works shall praise You, Lord our God,
and Your pious and righteous ones who do Your will
and Your people, the House of Israel,
will all tumultuously thank, bless
praise and flatter Your glorious Name.
For it is good to thank You,

בִּרְכַּת הַשִּׁיר

יש מנהגים שונים לגבי פירוש ברכת השיר.
מנהג הרמב"ם היא כשיטת רב יהודה:

יְהַלְלוּךָ יהוה אֱלֹהֵינוּ כָּל מַעֲשֶׂיךָ

וַחֲסִידֶיךָ וְצַדִּיקִים עוֹשֵׂי רְצוֹנֶךָ

וְכָל עַמְּךָ בֵּית יִשְׂרָאֵל

בְּרִנָּה יוֹדוּ לְשִׁמְךָ

כִּי אַתָּה יהוה

לְךָ טוֹב לְהוֹדוֹת

וּלְשִׁמְךָ נָעִים לְזַמֵּר

וּמֵעוֹלָם וְעַד עוֹלָם אַתָּה הָאֵל.

בָּרוּךְ אַתָּה יהוה, הַמֶּלֶךְ הַמְשֻׁבָּח הַמְפֹאָר

חַי וְקַיָּם, תָּמִיד יִמְלֹךְ לְעוֹלָם וָעֶד.

ומברכים על הכוס ושותים.

ורבי יוחנן אומר שברכת השיר היא נשמת כל חי. ויש אומרים שהיא שתיהם, ועוד מחלוקת מה קודם למה ובמה חותמים. ומנהג אשכנז הוא לומר יהללוך בלי חתימה ואחר כך נשמת:

ברכת השיר

יְהַלְלוּךָ יהוה אֱלֹהֵינוּ כָּל מַעֲשֶׂיךָ

וַחֲסִידֶיךָ וְצַדִּיקִים עוֹשֵׂי רְצוֹנֶךָ

וְעַמְּךָ בֵּית יִשְׂרָאֵל

כֻּלָּם בְּרִנָּה יוֹדוּ וִיבָרְכוּ

וִישַׁבְּחוּ וִיפָאֲרוּ אֶת שֵׁם כְּבוֹדֶךָ.

כִּי לְךָ טוֹב לְהוֹדוֹת

Hallel

To He Who made great luminaries
    for His kindness is forever.
The sun to rule by day   for His kindness is forever.
The moon and stars to rule by night
    for His kindness is forever.
To He Who smote Egypt through their firstborns
    for His kindness is forever.
He brought out Israel from their midst
    for His kindness is forever.
With a mighty hand and an outstretched arm
    for His kindness is forever.
To He Who split the Reed Sea asunder
    for His kindness is forever.
And took Israel through it   for His kindness is forever.
And tossed Pharaoh and his soldiers into the Reed Sea
    for His kindness is forever.
To He Who led His people through the wilderness
    for His kindness is forever.
To He Who smote great kings for His kindness is forever.
He slew mighty kings   for His kindness is forever.
Like Sihon, king of the Amorites
    for His kindness is forever.
And Og king of the Bashan   for His kindness is forever.
And He gave their land as an inheritance
    for His kindness is forever.
An inheritance for His servant Israel
    for His kindness is forever.
Who remembered us when we were at our low
    for His kindness is forever.
And delivered us from our oppressors
    for His kindness is forever.
He gives food to all flesh   for His kindness is forever.
Thank the God of heaven   for His kindness is forever.

לְעֹשֵׂה אוֹרִים גְּדֹלִים	כִּי לְעוֹלָם חַסְדּוֹ.
אֶת הַשֶּׁמֶשׁ לְמֶמְשֶׁלֶת בַּיּוֹם	כִּי לְעוֹלָם חַסְדּוֹ.
אֶת הַיָּרֵחַ וְכוֹכָבִים לְמֶמְשְׁלוֹת בַּלָּיְלָה	
	כִּי לְעוֹלָם חַסְדּוֹ.
לְמַכֵּה מִצְרַיִם בִּבְכוֹרֵיהֶם	כִּי לְעוֹלָם חַסְדּוֹ.
וַיּוֹצֵא יִשְׂרָאֵל מִתּוֹכָם	כִּי לְעוֹלָם חַסְדּוֹ.
בְּיָד חֲזָקָה וּבִזְרוֹעַ נְטוּיָה	כִּי לְעוֹלָם חַסְדּוֹ.
לְגֹזֵר יַם סוּף לִגְזָרִים	כִּי לְעוֹלָם חַסְדּוֹ.
וְהֶעֱבִיר יִשְׂרָאֵל בְּתוֹכוֹ	כִּי לְעוֹלָם חַסְדּוֹ.
וְנִעֵר פַּרְעֹה וְחֵילוֹ בְיַם סוּף	כִּי לְעוֹלָם חַסְדּוֹ.
לְמוֹלִיךְ עַמּוֹ בַּמִּדְבָּר	כִּי לְעוֹלָם חַסְדּוֹ.
לְמַכֵּה מְלָכִים גְּדֹלִים	כִּי לְעוֹלָם חַסְדּוֹ.
וַיַּהֲרֹג מְלָכִים אַדִּירִים	כִּי לְעוֹלָם חַסְדּוֹ.
לְסִיחוֹן מֶלֶךְ הָאֱמֹרִי	כִּי לְעוֹלָם חַסְדּוֹ.
וּלְעוֹג מֶלֶךְ הַבָּשָׁן	כִּי לְעוֹלָם חַסְדּוֹ.
וְנָתַן אַרְצָם לְנַחֲלָה	כִּי לְעוֹלָם חַסְדּוֹ.
נַחֲלָה לְיִשְׂרָאֵל עַבְדּוֹ	כִּי לְעוֹלָם חַסְדּוֹ.
שֶׁבְּשִׁפְלֵנוּ זָכַר לָנוּ	כִּי לְעוֹלָם חַסְדּוֹ.
וַיִּפְרְקֵנוּ מִצָּרֵינוּ	כִּי לְעוֹלָם חַסְדּוֹ.
נֹתֵן לֶחֶם לְכָל בָּשָׂר	כִּי לְעוֹלָם חַסְדּוֹ.
הוֹדוּ לְאֵל הַשָּׁמַיִם	כִּי לְעוֹלָם חַסְדּוֹ.

הלל

The Lord made this day; let us rejoice and be glad on it.
The Lord made this day; let us rejoice and be glad on it.
Please, O Lord, save us now!
　　　　　　　　　　　Please, O Lord, grant us success now!
Please, O Lord, save us now!　　　　Please, O Lord, grant us success now!
Blessed is he who comes in the name of the Lord
　　　　we blessed you from the house of the Lord.
Blessed is he who comes in the name of the Lord
　　　　　　　　　　　we blessed you from the house of the Lord.
The Lord is God, and He has illuminated for us;
Bind the festival offering with ropes,
　　　　　　　　　　　even to the horns of the altar.
The Lord is God, and He has illuminated for us;
Bind the festival offering with ropes,　　　even to the horns of the altar.
You are my God, and I will thank You;
　　　　　　　　　　　my God, I will exalt You.
You are my God, and I will thank You;　　　my God, I will exalt You.
Thank the Lord, for it is good;
　　　　　　　　　　　for His kindness is forever.
Thank the Lord, for it is good;　　　for His kindness is forever.

According to Maimonides, one can omit the following psalm, known to the sages as the Great Hallel, at this point, and after drinking the fourth cup of wine that is drunk after Birkat Hashir, fill a fifth cup, recite this psalm upon it, and then drink that fifth cup. Rabbis Menachem Mendel Kasher and Yisrael Rosen encouraged the practice in anticipation of the final Redemption; it is even more pertinent for those who have lived to see the Redemption.

Thank the Lord, for it is good
　　　　　　　　for His kindness is forever.
Thank the God of gods　　**for His kindness is forever.**
Thank the Lord of lords　　**for His kindness is forever.**
To He Who does great wonders by Himself
　　　　　　　　for His kindness is forever.
To He Who made the heavens through understanding
　　　　　　　　for His kindness is forever.
To He Who spread the earth upon the waters,
　　　　　　　　for His kindness is forever.

זֶה הַיּוֹם עָשָׂה יהוה	נָגִילָה וְנִשְׂמְחָה בוֹ.
זֶה הַיּוֹם עָשָׂה יהוה	נָגִילָה וְנִשְׂמְחָה בוֹ.
אָנָּא יהוה, הוֹשִׁיעָה נָּא.	אָנָּא יהוה, הַצְלִיחָה נָּא.
אָנָּא יהוה, הוֹשִׁיעָה נָּא.	אָנָּא יהוה, הַצְלִיחָה נָּא.
בָּרוּךְ הַבָּא בְּשֵׁם יהוה	בֵּרַכְנוּכֶם מִבֵּית יהוה.
בָּרוּךְ הַבָּא בְּשֵׁם יהוה	בֵּרַכְנוּכֶם מִבֵּית יהוה.
אֵל יהוה וַיָּאֶר לָנוּ;	
אִסְרוּ חַג בַּעֲבֹתִים	עַד קַרְנוֹת הַמִּזְבֵּחַ.
אֵל יהוה וַיָּאֶר לָנוּ;	
אִסְרוּ חַג בַּעֲבֹתִים	עַד קַרְנוֹת הַמִּזְבֵּחַ.
אֵלִי אַתָּה וְאוֹדֶךָּ	אֱלֹהַי אֲרוֹמְמֶךָּ.
אֵלִי אַתָּה וְאוֹדֶךָּ	אֱלֹהַי אֲרוֹמְמֶךָּ.
הוֹדוּ לַיהוה כִּי טוֹב	כִּי לְעוֹלָם חַסְדּוֹ.
הוֹדוּ לַיהוה כִּי טוֹב	כִּי לְעוֹלָם חַסְדּוֹ.

לפי הרמב"ם יש לו לדלג על הקטע הבא ולמזוג ולשתות עליו כוס חמישי אחרי ברכת השיר בסיום ההלל. וכתבו הרב מ"מ כשר והרב ישראל רוזן שבימינו ראוי לכולם להנהוג כן, קל וחומר בקץ הגאולה.

הוֹדוּ לַיהוה כִּי טוֹב	**כִּי לְעוֹלָם חַסְדּוֹ.**
הוֹדוּ לֵאלֹהֵי הָאֱלֹהִים	**כִּי לְעוֹלָם חַסְדּוֹ.**
הוֹדוּ לַאֲדֹנֵי הָאֲדֹנִים	**כִּי לְעוֹלָם חַסְדּוֹ.**
לְעֹשֵׂה נִפְלָאוֹת גְּדֹלוֹת לְבַדּוֹ	**כִּי לְעוֹלָם חַסְדּוֹ.**
לְעֹשֵׂה הַשָּׁמַיִם בִּתְבוּנָה	**כִּי לְעוֹלָם חַסְדּוֹ.**
לְרוֹקַע הָאָרֶץ עַל הַמָּיִם	**כִּי לְעוֹלָם חַסְדּוֹ.**

It is better to take refuge in the Lord
    than to trust in man.
It is better to take refuge in the Lord
    than to trust in dignitaries.
All nations surround me;
    I will cut them off with the name of the Lord.
They surround me all about;
    I will cut them off with the name of the Lord.
They surround me like bees;
they are squashed like the fire to thorns;
    I will cut them off with the name of the Lord.
You pushed me very hard so that I would fall,
    but the Lord helped me.
The Lord is my strength and song
    and He became my salvation.
A voice of rejoicing and salvation is in the tents of the righteous;   the Lord's right hand does valor.
The Lord's right hand is exalted;
    the Lord's right hand does valor.
I shall not die, but rather live,
    and I will tell of the Lord's deeds.
The Lord has severely chastened me
    but He has not given me over to death.
Open the gates of righteousness for me;
    I will enter by them; I will thank the Lord.
This is the gate of the Lord;
    the righteous shall enter by it.
I will thank You for You have answered me
    and You became my salvation.
I will thank You for You have answered me   and You became my salvation.
The stone rejected by the builders
    became the main corner-stone.
The stone rejected by the builders   became the main corner-stone.
This has come about by the Lord;
    it is amazing in our eyes.
This has come about by the Lord;   it is amazing in our eyes.

הלל

טוֹב לַחֲסוֹת בַּיהוה　　　　　　מִבְּטֹחַ בָּאָדָם.
טוֹב לַחֲסוֹת בַּיהוה　　　　　　מִבְּטֹחַ בִּנְדִיבִים.
כָּל גּוֹיִם סְבָבוּנִי　　　　　　בְּשֵׁם יהוה כִּי אֲמִילַם.
סַבּוּנִי גַם סְבָבוּנִי　　　　　　בְּשֵׁם יהוה כִּי אֲמִילַם.
סַבּוּנִי כִדְבֹרִים, דֹּעֲכוּ כְּאֵשׁ קוֹצִים
בְּשֵׁם יהוה כִּי אֲמִילַם.
דָּחֹה דְחִיתַנִי לִנְפֹּל　　　　　　וַיהוה עֲזָרָנִי.
עָזִּי וְזִמְרָת יָהּ　　　　　　וַיְהִי לִי לִישׁוּעָה.
קוֹל רִנָּה וִישׁוּעָה בְּאָהֳלֵי צַדִּיקִים
יְמִין יהוה עֹשָׂה חָיִל.
יְמִין יהוה רוֹמֵמָה　　　　　　יְמִין יהוה עֹשָׂה חָיִל.
לֹא אָמוּת כִּי אֶחְיֶה　　　　　　וַאֲסַפֵּר מַעֲשֵׂי יָהּ.
יַסֹּר יִסְּרַנִּי יָּהּ　　　　　　וְלַמָּוֶת לֹא נְתָנָנִי.
פִּתְחוּ לִי שַׁעֲרֵי צֶדֶק　　　　　　אָבֹא בָם אוֹדֶה יָהּ.
זֶה הַשַּׁעַר לַיהוה　　　　　　צַדִּיקִים יָבֹאוּ בוֹ.
אוֹדְךָ כִּי עֲנִיתָנִי　　　　　　וַתְּהִי לִי לִישׁוּעָה.
　　אוֹדְךָ כִּי עֲנִיתָנִי　　וַתְּהִי לִי לִישׁוּעָה.
אֶבֶן מָאֲסוּ הַבּוֹנִים　　　　　　הָיְתָה לְרֹאשׁ פִּנָּה.
　　אֶבֶן מָאֲסוּ הַבּוֹנִים　　הָיְתָה לְרֹאשׁ פִּנָּה.
מֵאֵת יהוה הָיְתָה זֹּאת　　　　　　הִיא נִפְלָאת בְּעֵינֵינוּ.
　　מֵאֵת יהוה הָיְתָה זֹּאת　　הִיא נִפְלָאת בְּעֵינֵינוּ.

sacrifice offered thereon is no different from that of the first day. (No musaf of Tabernacles is identical to that of any of the other days of the festival.)

We thus see that Hallel would have been appropriate for the latter days of Passover if not for this perplexing technical issue brought by the sages: those days do not have sacrifices sufficiently special to distinguish them from their brothers. (In truth, the musaf of every day of Passover happens to be identical to that of every New Moon and the day of Pentecost: two bulls, one ram, and seven lambs as a burnt offering and a he-goat as a sin-offering. For whatever reason, the musaf of the first day of Passover and the day of Pentecost is "novel" enough for this standard, but the musaf of the second day of Passover is already considered un-novel.) With regards to Hanukka, which is not biblical, and on which all manner of work is still permitted, we are forced to answer that we do as the sages decreed, and for whatever reason they saw fit to command us to recite Hallel then. We must also note that although a classic Midrash brings an aggadic reason for not reciting Hallel on Passover: God, so to speak, chastised the ministering angels for singing His praises while His handiwork was drowning in the sea, this was not utilized by the sages to decide the halacha. It is hard to explain why latter-day authorities suggested this as the reason for not reciting the complete Hallel on the latter days of Passover.

Returning to Rav and his reaction to the Babylonians' reciting half Hallel on the New Moon, we can suggest that Rav tolerated their novel practice because he already was familiar with another, similar practice of reciting an incomplete Hallel on the days that although no one completes the Hallel thereon, because they are holidays and meet other criteria, it is appropriate for something to be recited, and those days were none other than the latter six days of Passover. This explains, for example, why the sages in Arachin describe days on which we complete the Hallel, because they were implying that there are days when Hallel is recited, just not completely, and also why the medieval authorities assumed a universal custom of reciting the abridged Hallel on Passover.

Thank the Lord, for it is good;   for His kindness is forever.
Let Israel say it   for His kindness is forever.
Let the house of Aaron say it   for His kindness is forever.
Let those who fear the Lord say it

                                for His kindness is forever.
I called the Lord from the strait;
                               God answered me with an expanse.
The Lord is mine; I will not fear.
                               What can man do to me?
The Lord is mine, among my helpers,
                               and I shall look upon my haters.

However, we should ask, where is the Talmudic source for the practice to recite half Hallel on the latter six days of Passover? Further, why did the sages initially use the term "completing" the Hallel in the aforementioned teaching from Arachin? After all, with regard to the mandated recitations of other biblical passages, like the daily sh'ma and the public Torah and Megilla readings, they used terms like "reading" or "recitation"! Even today, there are some versions that read "Who has sanctified us with His commandments, and commanded us to recite/read the Hallel," and some read, "and commanded us to complete the Hallel." Further, why was Rav satisfied with the fact that the Babylonians started leaving out sections of the Hallel if the problem was that they were reciting Hallel in any event on a day on which there was no commandment to do so? After all, the sages have taught us that whoever recites the Hallel every day, is basically declaring a brazen blasphemy, so why would it have helped that they skipped sections? According to those who claim that the Babylonians even recited a blessing before this novel, truncated Hallel, the question is even more serious. They should have just not been saying Hallel to begin with, let alone reciting an unnecessary and untruthful blessing.

Rather, we need to look more deeply into the sages' words in Arachin, above, that there are days when we complete the Hallel and why. The weekly Sabbath is neither one of the appointed times that depend on the rest of the Jewish calendar, nor a day of rejoicing, so we do not recite the Hallel thereon. The Hallel is also not recited in full on New Moons because they are not days that are sanctified with a prohibition against the performance of Talmudically-defined work, although they are days on which a special, additional sacrifice is offered in the Temple. (See the next book in this series, *Hahodesh Hazeh Lachem*, for an explanation as to why the Babylonians began to recite the Hallel on Rosh Hodesh.) Hallel is inappropriate for Rosh Hashana and Yom Kippur because they are days of judgment (and dread). However, the eight days of Tabernacles, the first day of Passover, and the day of Pentecost are biblical holidays on which work is prohibited, are days of rejoicing and additional sacrifices in the Temple, and are the paradigms for days appropriate for Hallel, while the latter six days of Passover are less special in that the special

הלל

הוֹדוּ לַיהוה כִּי טוֹב	כִּי לְעוֹלָם חַסְדּוֹ.
יֹאמַר נָא יִשְׂרָאֵל	כִּי לְעוֹלָם חַסְדּוֹ.
יֹאמְרוּ נָא בֵית אַהֲרֹן	כִּי לְעוֹלָם חַסְדּוֹ.
יֹאמְרוּ נָא יִרְאֵי יהוה	כִּי לְעוֹלָם חַסְדּוֹ.
מִן הַמֵּצַר קָרָאתִי יָּהּ	עָנָנִי בַמֶּרְחָב יָהּ.
יהוה לִי, לֹא אִירָא	מַה יַּעֲשֶׂה לִי אָדָם.
יהוה לִי בְּעֹזְרָי	וַאֲנִי אֶרְאֶה בְשֹׂנְאָי.

| Grave in the Lord's eyes | is the death of His pious ones. |
| Please, O Lord, | for I am Your servant; |

I am Your servant, the son of Your handmaid;
                You have released my restraints.
I will offer a thanksgiving sacrifice to You
                and call in the Lord's name.
I will fulfill my vows to the Lord
                in the presence of His entire people,
In the courtyards of the Lord's house
                in your midst, O Jerusalem.
Hallelujah!

Praise the Lord, all you nations;
                laud Him, all you peoples.
For His kindness has overwhelmed us
                and the Lord's truth is forever.
Hallelujah!

However, in Ta'anit 28 we learn about how when Rav left Israel for Babylonia after the death of Rabbi Judah the Prince, he found the Babylonian Jews reciting the Hallel on the New Moon, and he sought to stop them from doing so, but when he realized they were skipping sections, he became tolerant of their surprising practice. This incident serves as the source for the now widespread custom of reciting the Hallel on New Moons. From the medieval authorities, we learn that there is also a practice to recite the abridged, or "half," Hallel on the latter days of Passover in the manner of the abridged Hallel recited on New Moons, while the same authorities dispute whether a blessing is recited before the abridged Hallel. Rabbeinu Tam inferred from the aforementioned story of Rav's arrival in Babylonia that the people recited a blessing before the Hallel, even though there was neither a biblical nor a rabbinic commandment to recite Hallel then, while Maimonides and others inferred that a blessing should not be recited before such a Hallel. Others left the matter of a prefatory blessing to the will of the congregation, while still others reasoned that a blessing on half Hallel is appropriate specifically on Passover because it is a festival of redemption. Lastly, there were those who argued that a blessing on the abridged Hallel was appropriate for the New Moon because of the great importance of publicizing the day the court had decided to establish as the starting point for that calendar month, which is the basis for all of the holidays. Thus, every possible practice has its authoritative exponents.

הַמָּוְתָה לַחֲסִידָיו.	יָקָר בְּעֵינֵי יהוה
כִּי אֲנִי עַבְדֶּךָ;	אָנָּא יהוה
פִּתַּחְתָּ לְמוֹסֵרָי.	אֲנִי עַבְדְּךָ בֶּן אֲמָתֶךָ
וּבְשֵׁם יהוה אֶקְרָא.	לְךָ אֶזְבַּח זֶבַח תּוֹדָה
נֶגְדָה נָּא לְכָל עַמּוֹ.	נְדָרַי לַיהוה אֲשַׁלֵּם
בְּתוֹכֵכִי יְרוּשָׁלָיִם.	בְּחַצְרוֹת בֵּית יהוה
	הַלְלוּיָהּ!

שַׁבְּחוּהוּ כָּל הָאֻמִּים.	הַלְלוּ אֶת יהוה כָּל גּוֹיִם
וֶאֱמֶת יהוה לְעוֹלָם.	כִּי גָבַר עָלֵינוּ חַסְדּוֹ
	הַלְלוּיָהּ!

As we saw in the introduction, Hallel is recited during the offering of the Pesah, during the seder, and as part of the prayers on the first day of Yom Tov, but on the latter six days of the festival, during Hol Hamo'ed and the seventh day of Passover, Hallel is not recited. On the tenth folio of Arachin, it is mentioned that Rabbi Johanan said in Rabbi Simon ben Jehozadak's name that there are eighteen days during the year when the complete Hallel is recited: The eight days of Tabernacles, the eight days of Hanukka, the first day of Passover, and the single day of Pentecost. The preceding Mishna lists those days when the Hallel is recited in the Temple, while Rabbi Johanan lists those days on which the Hallel is part of the prayers, explaining why, for example, Hallel is not recited on Hanukka in the Temple: since the holiday is a rabbinic enactment, it has no special offering which could be accompanied by the Levites' singing the Hallel, whereas on the fourteenth of Nisan, when the Pesah is offered in the Temple, they do sing Hallel, although outside of the Temple, Hallel is not recited because the day is a (not-so-)ordinary weekday. During the exile, in order to memorialize how the Levites would sing the Hallel when the Pesah was offered, there was a custom to recite the Hallel while baking the matzot that would be eaten at the Seder in memory of the consumption of the Pesah.

The Talmud, above, concludes that Hallel is not recited on ordinary Sabbaths, New Moons, Rosh Hashana, Yom Kippur, or the latter six days of Passover.

You are blessed of the Lord,   Maker of heaven and earth.
The heavens are the heavens of the Lord,
	but He has given the earth to the children of man.
The dead will not praise the Lord,
	and neither do any who descend to eternal silence;
But we will bless the Lord   from now and until forever.
Hallelujah!

I loved that the Lord would hear
	my voice, my supplications.
That He has lent His ear to me
	and I will call [Him] all my days.
The cords of death surrounded me, and the straits of the underworld found me;   I found trouble and sorrow,
But I will call upon the name of the Lord;
	Please, O Lord, save my soul.
The Lord is gracious and righteous
	and our God is merciful.
The Lord protects the simple;
	I became impoverished, and He saved me.
Return, my soul, to your place of rest,
	for the Lord has dealt well with you.
For You have delivered my soul from death,
my eyes from tears,   and my feet from faltering.
I will walk before the Lord   in the lands of the living.
I trusted when I spoke: "I was very distraught."
I said in my haste: 'All mankind is deceptive.'
How can I compensate the Lord
	for all the good He dealt to me?
I will raise the cup of salvation,
	and call in the Lord's name.
I will fulfill my vows to the Lord
	in the presence of His entire people.

בְּרוּכִים אַתֶּם לַיהוה	עֹשֵׂה שָׁמַיִם וָאָרֶץ.
הַשָּׁמַיִם שָׁמַיִם לַיהוה	וְהָאָרֶץ נָתַן לִבְנֵי אָדָם.
לֹא הַמֵּתִים יְהַלְלוּ יָהּ	וְלֹא כָּל יֹרְדֵי דוּמָה.
וַאֲנַחְנוּ נְבָרֵךְ יָהּ	מֵעַתָּה וְעַד עוֹלָם.
הַלְלוּיָהּ!	

אָהַבְתִּי כִּי יִשְׁמַע יהוה	אֶת קוֹלִי תַּחֲנוּנָי.
כִּי הִטָּה אָזְנוֹ לִי	וּבְיָמַי אֶקְרָא.
אֲפָפוּנִי חֶבְלֵי מָוֶת, וּמְצָרֵי שְׁאוֹל מְצָאוּנִי	
צָרָה וְיָגוֹן אֶמְצָא.	
וּבְשֵׁם יהוה אֶקְרָא	אָנָּא יהוה מַלְּטָה נַפְשִׁי.
חַנּוּן יהוה וְצַדִּיק	וֵאלֹהֵינוּ מְרַחֵם.
שֹׁמֵר פְּתָאיִם יהוה	דַּלֹּתִי וְלִי יְהוֹשִׁיעַ.
שׁוּבִי נַפְשִׁי לִמְנוּחָיְכִי	כִּי יהוה גָּמַל עָלָיְכִי.
כִּי חִלַּצְתָּ נַפְשִׁי מִמָּוֶת;	
אֶת עֵינִי מִן דִּמְעָה	אֶת רַגְלִי מִדֶּחִי.
אֶתְהַלֵּךְ לִפְנֵי יהוה	בְּאַרְצוֹת הַחַיִּים.
הֶאֱמַנְתִּי כִּי אֲדַבֵּר	אֲנִי עָנִיתִי מְאֹד.
אֲנִי אָמַרְתִּי בְחָפְזִי	כָּל הָאָדָם כֹּזֵב.
מָה אָשִׁיב לַיהוה	כָּל תַּגְמוּלוֹהִי עָלָי.
כּוֹס יְשׁוּעוֹת אֶשָּׂא	וּבְשֵׁם יהוה אֶקְרָא.
נְדָרַי לַיהוה אֲשַׁלֵּם	נֶגְדָה נָּא לְכָל עַמּוֹ.

הלל

and, to complete the analogy, the matza and wine they consume with the Pesah are the meal offerings and libations that accompany the sacrifice, while the Hallel that we are about to recite is in place of the Levitic song that should accompany any other public sacrifice. Therefore, because the drinking of the four cups and the recitation of the Hallel are not commandments in their own right, unlike the matza or maror, for example, which are their own commandments, we do not recite a blessing before their performance. We see how our sages therefore enacted that Hallel be recited both during the Passover service in the Temple and during the Passover service in the sanctuaries that are the Jewish homes.

Not to us, O Lord, not to us,
but rather give glory to Your Name
  for Your kindnesses, and for Your truth's sake.
Why should the nations say "Where is their God?"
But our God is in the heavens;
  He has done all that He pleased.
Their idols are silver and gold,
  pieces of man's handiwork.
They have a mouth, but they do not speak;
  they have eyes, but they do not see;
they have ears, but they do not hear;
  they have a nose, but they do not smell.
They have hands, but they do not feel;
they have feet, but they do not walk;
  they do not articulate with their throat.
They that make them shall be like them;
  everyone who trusts in them.
Israel, trust in the Lord! **He is their helper and shield!**
House of Aaron, trust in the Lord!
  He is their helper and shield!
You who fear the Lord, trust in the Lord!
  He is their helper and shield.
The Lord has remembered us; He will bless –
He will bless the house of Israel;
  He will bless the house of Aaron;
He will bless those who fear the Lord,
  both the minor and the great.
May the Lord increase your numbers,
  yours and your children's.

he is ritually pure, whereas the ones who register to eat of a particular Korban Pesah must eat from that Pesah and no others may do so, just like the priests officially on duty on any given day are the only ones who eat from the priestly portions from that day's sacrificial service. Indeed, although the priests receive specific portions from the peace offerings, the Aaronite priests receive no portion in particular from the Pesah brought by non-priests, because, in the case of the Pesah, all of the people are like priests, and the priests are just as obligated as everyone else to bring their own Pesahim. The sages said that with regard to the priestly portions, the priests eat the meat, while those who brought the sacrifice attain atonement. Instead, with regard to the Korban Pesah, the participants who eat the Pesah are the priests,

הלל

לֹא לָנוּ, יהוה, לֹא לָנוּ;
כִּי לְשִׁמְךָ תֵּן כָּבוֹד עַל חַסְדְּךָ עַל אֲמִתֶּךָ.
לָמָּה יֹאמְרוּ הַגּוֹיִם אַיֵּה נָא אֱלֹהֵיהֶם.
וֵאלֹהֵינוּ בַשָּׁמָיִם כֹּל אֲשֶׁר חָפֵץ עָשָׂה.
עֲצַבֵּיהֶם כֶּסֶף וְזָהָב מַעֲשֵׂה יְדֵי אָדָם.
פֶּה לָהֶם וְלֹא יְדַבֵּרוּ עֵינַיִם לָהֶם וְלֹא יִרְאוּ.
אָזְנַיִם לָהֶם וְלֹא יִשְׁמָעוּ אַף לָהֶם וְלֹא יְרִיחוּן.
יְדֵיהֶם וְלֹא יְמִישׁוּן, רַגְלֵיהֶם וְלֹא יְהַלֵּכוּ
לֹא יֶהְגּוּ בִּגְרוֹנָם.
כְּמוֹהֶם יִהְיוּ עֹשֵׂיהֶם כֹּל אֲשֶׁר בֹּטֵחַ בָּהֶם.
יִשְׂרָאֵל בְּטַח בַּיהוה עֶזְרָם וּמָגִנָּם הוּא.
בֵּית אַהֲרֹן בִּטְחוּ בַיהוה עֶזְרָם וּמָגִנָּם הוּא.
יִרְאֵי יהוה בִּטְחוּ בַיהוה עֶזְרָם וּמָגִנָּם הוּא.
יהוה זְכָרָנוּ יְבָרֵךְ;
יְבָרֵךְ אֶת בֵּית יִשְׂרָאֵל יְבָרֵךְ אֶת בֵּית אַהֲרֹן.
יְבָרֵךְ יִרְאֵי יהוה הַקְּטַנִּים עִם הַגְּדֹלִים.
יֹסֵף יהוה עֲלֵיכֶם עֲלֵיכֶם וְעַל בְּנֵיכֶם.

They will turn as one shoulder to serve You
    and those who seek Your countenance shall fear You.
They will recognize Your kingdom's power
    and those who stray will learn understanding.
They will speak of Your might
    and they will exalt You above the highest exultations.
They will recoil in fear from Your countenance
    and crown You with a splendid diadem.
The mountains will burst with commotion
    and islands will shout when You reign.
They will accept the yoke of Your kingdom
    and elevate You in huge crowds.
The distant will hear, and come
    and they will give a royal crown to You.

devoured Jacob, and laid his habitation waste. Pour Your fury upon them, and let the fierceness of Your anger overtake them. Pursue them in anger, and eliminate them from under the heavens of the Lord."

Hallel

The fourth cup is poured, and the recitation of the Hallel is completed. From this point, the participants no longer have to stay in each other's company or within the room, and may choose to complete the recitation of the Hallel wherever they wish.

should be accompanied by a Levitic song, why didn't the Torah obligate us to bring the Korban Pesah along with complementary libations (and meal offerings)? It is also proper to address two other, classic questions regarding the seder: Why is there no blessing recited on this recitation of Hallel, "Who has sanctified us with His commandments, and commanded us to recite the Hallel," that normally is recited before any other obligatory recitation of Hallel? Secondly, why is there no similar blessing preceding the rabbinic commandment to drink the four cups?

It seems, based on what we have seen earlier, that the Passover sacrifice is unlike all the other peace offerings that are consumed by non-priests. Ordinary peace offerings are not accompanied by a Levitic song because they are those of individuals, whereas the Pesah is a public offering, and requires an accompanying song. Those who partake of the Korban Pesah are not analogous to those who are invited by the one making the peace offering to join in his celebratory meal. Anyone can join in the consumption of the latter, even the night after the sacrificial service, as long as

וְיִטּוּ שְׁכֶם אֶחָד לְעָבְדֶּךָ	וְיִרְאוּךָ מְבַקְשֵׁי פָנֶיךָ
וְיַכִּירוּ כֹּחַ מַלְכוּתֶךָ	וְיִלְמְדוּ תּוֹעִים בִּינָה
וִימַלְּלוּ אֶת גְּבוּרָתֶךָ	וְיִנַּשְּׂאוּךָ מִתְנַשֵּׂא לְכֹל לְרֹאשׁ
וִיסַלְּדוּ בְחִילָה פָנֶיךָ	וִיעַטְּרוּךָ נֵזֶר תִּפְאָרָה
וְיִפְצְחוּ הָרִים רִנָּה	וְיִצְהֲלוּ אִיִּים בְּמָלְכֶךָ
וִיקַבְּלוּ עֹל מַלְכוּתֶךָ	וִירוֹמְמוּךָ בִּקְהַל עָם
וְיִשְׁמְעוּ רְחוֹקִים וְיָבוֹאוּ	וְיִתְּנוּ לְךָ כֶּתֶר מְלוּכָה.

During the dark days of the exile, the custom was to pray at this point for the destruction of the Jewish people's enemies: "Pour Your wrath upon the nations that do not know You, and on the kingdoms that do not call Your name. For they have

מוזגים כוס רביעי, וגומרים עליו את ההלל.
מכאן ואילך, רשאים בני החבורה להיפרד זה מזה ולצאת מן החדר ולומר
ההלל והפיוטים בטוב בעיניהם.

Maimonides writes that the entire time that the throngs in the Temple are slaughtering and sacrificing the Pesah, the Levites recite the Hallel, which is sometimes repeated once or twice due to the length of time the sacrificing takes, and that they accompany every recitation with three soundings of the trumpets – *t'kia, t'ruah, t'kia* – because normally, the trumpets are sounded when a particular sacrifice's libation is offered, but because the Pesah has no accompanying libation, they sound the trumpets during the time of the Pesah's slaughter.

Maimonides also writes that the Levites would only sing when the priests brought the libations that accompany the obligatory public burnt offerings and the peace offerings of Pentecost, but that they do not sing on those occasions when public burnt offerings are brought solely in order that the altar not remain idle on a day when there are few pilgrims bringing sacrifice, referred to as *ketz hamizbeah*, nor do the Levites sing when libations are brought independent of animal sacrifice. It seems, therefore, that the question should be, if it is assumed that the Korban Pesah

have trouble accepting this because my own great grandfather was renowned for his scholarship and piety, and it was well-known that Elijah would actually drink from his cup, as everyone saw the wine go down.

The door to the outside is opened, and the following prayer for the reconciliation of the nations of the world with their Creator is recited:

They shall not harm nor shall they destroy anywhere on My holy mountain, for the earth shall be full of the knowledge of the Lord as the waters cover the sea. It shall be on every New Moon and on every Sabbath that all flesh shall come to bow before Me said the Lord.

See the Introduction regarding the idea that the house in which the Pesah is eaten is like a sanctuary.

from the Malchuyot blessing of the musaf prayer of Rosh Hashana, commonly known as the Aleinu prayer:

We therefore hope that You, O Lord, our God, allow us speedily to behold the splendor of Your might… to establish the Kingdom of the Almighty throughout the world, and all flesh will call in Your name, causing all the wicked of the earth to turn to You. All the inhabitants of Earth will recognize and know that every knee shall bow to You, that every tongue will swear by You. Before You, O Lord, our God, they will bow and prostrate themselves, they will ascribe honor to Your glorious Name, and they will all accept upon themselves the yoke of Your kingdom, and may You soon reign over them forever and ever. Amen, so may it be His will.

All will come to serve You
    and they will bless your glorious Name.
They will speak of Your righteousness in the Islands
    and nations that know You not will seek you
All those throughout the world will praise You
    and they will constantly say, "may the Lord be magnified."
They will slaughter their sacrifices to You
    and they will ditch their detestations.

Rabbi Hershel Schachter says that it is inappropriate to teach children that Elijah the prophet actually enters the house and drinks from the cup, as it is reminiscent of the nonsense that the heathens customarily teach their children. However, I

פותחים את הדלת ואומרים תפלה למען אומות העולם שיחזרו לעבודת שמים:

לֹא־יָרֵעוּ וְלֹא־יַשְׁחִיתוּ בְּכָל הַר קָדְשִׁי
כִּי מָלְאָה הָאָרֶץ דֵּעָה אֶת יהוה
כַּמַּיִם לַיָּם מְכַסִּים.
וְהָיָה מִדֵּי־חֹדֶשׁ בְּחָדְשׁוֹ
וּמִדֵּי שַׁבָּת בְּשַׁבַּתּוֹ,
יָבוֹא כָל־בָּשָׂר לְהִשְׁתַּחֲוֹת לְפָנַי
אָמַר יהוה.

וראה בהקדמה לגבי ענין הבית בו אוכלים את הפסח כמקום המקדש.

During the exile, the goal of the Jewish people was to return to the land of Israel, while during the period of the ingathering of the exiles, the goal was to see to the rebuilding of the Temple and the return of the Divine Presence to Zion, but what is their goal once they have already been redeemed, and when the Temple is firmly established and Israel dwells securely? They will do as they did during the days of King Solomon, to serve as a beacon for the nations of the world and bring them to repent, for the sake of sanctifying the Name of Heaven. It is clear that the Jewish people were created to be the medium for shining the divine light upon the nations. This is the general vision of the prophets, and is understood

ברך

וְיֵאָתָיוּ כֹל לְעָבְדֶךָ   וִיבָרְכוּ שֵׁם כְּבוֹדֶךָ
וְיַגִּידוּ בָאִיִּים צִדְקֶךָ   וְיִדְרְשׁוּךָ עַמִּים לֹא יְדָעוּךָ
וִיהַלְלוּךָ כָּל אַפְסֵי אָרֶץ   וְיֹאמְרוּ תָמִיד יִגְדַּל יהוה
וְיִזְבְּחוּ לְךָ אֶת זִבְחֵיהֶם   וְיַחְפְּרוּ עִם עֲצַבֵּיהֶם

our Redeemer, our Fashioner, our Holy One,
the Holy One of Jacob,
our Shepherd, the Shepherd of Israel,
the good King Who does good to all,
Who, each and every day,
has done good, does good, and will do good for us.
He has granted, He grants,
and He will always grant us
with grace, kindness, and mercy,
relief, rescue, success, blessing,
salvation; consolation, livelihood, sustenance,
mercy, life, peace, and all good,
and He will never deprive us of any goodness.

May the Merciful One be praised for all generations,
pride Himself in us for all eternity,
and glorify Himself in us forever.
May the Merciful One provide for us in dignity.
May the Merciful One allow us to merit
the life of the World to Come.

Blessed are You, O Lord, our God,
King of the universe,
Creator of the fruit of the vine.

The third cup is then drunk, but the blessing that normally follows is recited later.

Some have the custom to pour a cup of wine in honor of Elijah the prophet at this point.

גְּאָלֵנוּ יוֹצְרֵנוּ קְדוֹשֵׁנוּ קְדוֹשׁ יַעֲקֹב
רוֹעֵנוּ רוֹעֵה יִשְׂרָאֵל
הַמֶּלֶךְ הַטּוֹב וְהַמֵּטִיב לַכֹּל
שֶׁבְּכָל יוֹם וָיוֹם
הוּא הֵטִיב, הוּא מֵטִיב, הוּא יֵיטִיב לָנוּ.
הוּא גְמָלָנוּ, הוּא גוֹמְלֵנוּ, הוּא יִגְמְלֵנוּ לָעַד
לְחֵן וּלְחֶסֶד וּלְרַחֲמִים
וּלְרֶוַח הַצָּלָה וְהַצְלָחָה, בְּרָכָה
וִישׁוּעָה נֶחָמָה פַּרְנָסָה וְכַלְכָּלָה
וְרַחֲמִים וְחַיִּים וְשָׁלוֹם וְכָל טוֹב
וּמִכָּל טוּב לְעוֹלָם עַל יְחַסְּרֵנוּ.

הָרַחֲמָן הוּא יִשְׁתַּבַּח לְדוֹר דּוֹרִים
וְיִתְפָּאַר בָּנוּ לָעַד וּלְנֵצַח נְצָחִים
וְיִתְהַדַּר בָּנוּ לָעַד וּלְעוֹלְמֵי עוֹלָמִים.
הָרַחֲמָן הוּא יְפַרְנְסֵנוּ בְּכָבוֹד.
הָרַחֲמָן הוּא יְזַכֵּנוּ לְחַיֵּי הָעוֹלָם הַבָּא.

ברך

בָּרוּךְ אַתָּה יהוה, אֱלֹהֵינוּ מֶלֶךְ הָעוֹלָם
בּוֹרֵא פְּרִי הַגָּפֶן.

ושותים, ואין לברך ברכה אחרונה.

יש נוהגים למזוג כוס לאליהו הנביא זכור לטוב.

Our God and our fathers' God,
may our memory and recollection,
the memory of our ancestors,
the memory of the Messiah,
scion of Your servant David,
the memory of Your holy city, Jerusalem,
and the memory of Your entire nation of Israel
ascend, arrive, reach, be seen,
be accepted, be heard, be recalled,
and be remembered
before You for deliverance, goodness,
grace, kindness, mercy,
life, and peace, on this day of the Festival of Matzot.
Remember us, O Lord, our God,
on this day for goodness,
and recall us on this day for a blessing,
and save us on this day for life.
With a message of salvation and mercy,
spare us, grace us, have mercy on us, and save us,
for our eyes look to You,
for You are a gracious and merciful God and King.

Blessed are You, O Lord, Builder of Jerusalem.
Amen.

Blessed are You, O Lord our God, King of the universe,
God, our Father, our King, our Might, our Creator,

אֱלֹהֵינוּ וֵאלֹהֵי אֲבוֹתֵינוּ
יַעֲלֶה וְיָבֹא וְיַגִּיעַ וְיֵרָאֶה
וְיֵרָצֶה וְיִשָּׁמַע וְיִפָּקֵד וְיִזָּכֵר
זִכְרוֹנֵנוּ וּפִקְדּוֹנֵנוּ, וְזִכְרוֹן אֲבוֹתֵינוּ
וְזִכְרוֹן מָשִׁיחַ בֶּן דָּוִד עַבְדֶּךָ
וְזִכְרוֹן יְרוּשָׁלַיִם עִיר קָדְשֶׁךָ
וְזִכְרוֹן כָּל עַמְּךָ בֵּית יִשְׂרָאֵל לְפָנֶיךָ
לִפְלֵיטָה לְטוֹבָה
לְחֵן וּלְחֶסֶד וּלְרַחֲמִים
לְחַיִּים וּלְשָׁלוֹם, בְּיוֹם חַג הַמַּצּוֹת הַזֶּה.
זָכְרֵנוּ, יהוה אֱלֹהֵינוּ, בּוֹ לְטוֹבָה
וּפָקְדֵנוּ בוֹ לִבְרָכָה
וְהוֹשִׁיעֵנוּ בוֹ לְחַיִּים.
וּבִדְבַר יְשׁוּעָה וְרַחֲמִים
חוּס וְחָנֵּנוּ וְרַחֵם עָלֵינוּ וְהוֹשִׁיעֵנוּ
כִּי אֵלֶיךָ עֵינֵינוּ
כִּי אֵל מֶלֶךְ חַנּוּן וְרַחוּם אָתָּה.

בָּרוּךְ אַתָּה יהוה, בּוֹנֵה יְרוּשָׁלָיִם. אָמֵן.

בָּרוּךְ אַתָּה יהוה, אֱלֹהֵינוּ מֶלֶךְ הָעוֹלָם
הָאֵל אָבִינוּ מַלְכֵּנוּ אַדִּירֵנוּ בּוֹרְאֵנוּ

Our God, our Father, tend us, sustain us
provide us, feed us, and relieve us;
relieve us, O Lord our God, speedily,
from all of our troubles.
Please, O Lord our God, do not make us depend
on the gifts of flesh and blood
or on their loans.
Rather, only on Your hand,
which is full, open, holy, and generous,
so that we will never be ashamed or disgraced.

On the Sabbath, the following paragraph is added:

Be pleased with us and strengthen us, O Lord, our God,
through Your commandments,
and through the commandment of the seventh say,
this great and holy Sabbath,
for this is a great and holy day before You,
to desist from work and to rest thereon with love,
in accordance with Your will's commandment.
May it be Your will, O Lord our God,
that You grant us rest,
that there be no distress, sorrow,
or moaning on our day of rest.

אֱלֹהֵינוּ אָבִינוּ, רְעֵנוּ זוּנֵנוּ
פַּרְנְסֵנוּ וְכַלְכְּלֵנוּ וְהַרְוִיחֵנוּ,
וְהַרְוַח לָנוּ יְהוָה אֱלֹהֵינוּ, מְהֵרָה מִכָּל צָרוֹתֵינוּ.
וְנָא אַל תַּצְרִיכֵנוּ יְהוָה אֱלֹהֵינוּ
לֹא לִידֵי מַתְּנַת בָּשָׂר וָדָם
וְלֹא לִידֵי הַלְוָאָתָם
כִּי אִם לְיָדְךָ
הַמְּלֵאָה הַפְּתוּחָה הַקְּדוֹשָׁה וְהָרְחָבָה
שֶׁלֹּא נֵבוֹשׁ וְלֹא נִכָּלֵם לְעוֹלָם וָעֶד.

בשבת מוסיפין:

רְצֵה וְהַחֲלִיצֵנוּ יְהוָה אֱלֹהֵינוּ בְּמִצְוֹתֶיךָ
וּבְמִצְוַת יוֹם הַשְּׁבִיעִי
הַשַּׁבָּת הַגָּדוֹל וְהַקָּדוֹשׁ הַזֶּה
כִּי יוֹם זֶה גָּדוֹל וְקָדוֹשׁ לְפָנֶיךָ
לִשְׁבָּת־בּוֹ וְלָנוּחַ בּוֹ
בְּאַהֲבָה כְּמִצְוַת רְצוֹנֶךָ.
וּבִרְצוֹנְךָ הָנִיחַ לָנוּ יְהוָה אֱלֹהֵינוּ
שֶׁלֹּא תְהֵא צָרָה וְיָגוֹן וַאֲנָחָה בְּיוֹם מְנוּחָתֵנוּ.

and for the consumption of the food You provide,
sustaining us constantly,
every day, and every time, and every hour.

For all this, O Lord our God,
we thank You and bless You.
May Your Name be blessed
by the mouth of all that live,
constantly and forever, as it is written:
You shall eat and be satiated,
and then you shall bless the Lord, your God
for the good land which He has given you.
Blessed are You, O Lord,
for the land and for the sustenance.

Bareich

Uphold for us, O Lord our God,
Your people Israel,
Your city, Jerusalem,
Zion, Your glorious abode,
the kingdom of the house of David, Your anointed,
and the great and holy Temple
dedicated to Your Name.

According to Rabbi Dov Lior, the language of this blessing during Temple times should reflect our hope that it and the Davidic dynasty persist, and that is reflected here and in the three-faceted blessing, below.

וְעַל אֲכִילַת מָזוֹן שָׁאַתָּה זָן
וּמְפַרְנֵס אוֹתָנוּ תָּמִיד
בְּכָל יוֹם, וּבְכָל עֵת, וּבְכָל שָׁעָה.

וְעַל הַכֹּל יהוה אֱלֹהֵינוּ
אֲנַחְנוּ מוֹדִים לָךְ וּמְבָרְכִים אוֹתָךְ
יִתְבָּרַךְ שִׁמְךָ בְּפִי כָּל חַי
תָּמִיד לְעוֹלָם וָעֶד, כַּכָּתוּב:
וְאָכַלְתָּ וְשָׂבָעְתָּ
וּבֵרַכְתָּ אֶת יהוה אֱלֹהֶיךָ
עַל הָאָרֶץ הַטּוֹבָה אֲשֶׁר נָתַן לָךְ.
בָּרוּךְ אַתָּה יהוה, עַל הָאָרֶץ וְעַל הַמָּזוֹן.

קַיֵּם לָנוּ יהוה אֱלֹהֵינוּ
אֶת יִשְׂרָאֵל עַמֶּךָ
וְאֶת יְרוּשָׁלַיִם עִירֶךָ
וְאֶת צִיּוֹן מִשְׁכַּן כְּבוֹדֶךָ
וְאֶת מַלְכוּת בֵּית דָּוִד מְשִׁיחֶךָ
וְאֶת הַבַּיִת הַגָּדוֹל וְהַקָּדוֹשׁ שֶׁנִּקְרָא שִׁמְךָ עָלָיו.

The Grace begins here:

**Blessed are You, O Lord, our God,
King of the universe,
Who sustains the entire world
through goodness, with grace,
with kindness, and with mercy.
He gives food to all flesh, for His kindness is forever.
Through His great goodness, we have never lacked
nor shall we ever lack sustenance.
For the sake of His great Name,
for He is a God who sustains and provides for all,
does good to all,
and prepares sustenance for all of His creatures
that He has created.
Blessed are You, O Lord,
Who sustains all.**

**We thank You, O Lord, our God,
for apportioning to us and our fathers
an enviable, good, and spacious land,
and for bringing us, O Lord, our God,
out of the land of Egypt,
and saving us from the house of bondage,
and for Your covenant which You sealed in our flesh,
and for Your Torah which You have taught us
and for Your statutes of which You have informed us,
and for the life, favor, and kindness
with which You have graced us,**

והמזמן ממשיך:

בָּרוּךְ אַתָּה יהוה, אֱלֹהֵינוּ מֶלֶךְ הָעוֹלָם
הַזָּן אֶת הָעוֹלָם כֻּלּוֹ
בְּטוּבוֹ, בְּחֵן, בְּחֶסֶד, וּבְרַחֲמִים
הוּא נוֹתֵן לֶחֶם לְכָל בָּשָׂר
כִּי לְעוֹלָם חַסְדּוֹ.
וּבְטוּבוֹ הַגָּדוֹל תָּמִיד לֹא חָסַר לָנוּ
וְאַל יֶחְסַר לָנוּ מָזוֹן לְעוֹלָם וָעֶד.
בַּעֲבוּר שְׁמוֹ הַגָּדוֹל
כִּי הוּא אֵל זָן וּמְפַרְנֵס לַכֹּל, וּמֵטִיב לַכֹּל
וּמֵכִין מָזוֹן לְכָל בְּרִיּוֹתָיו אֲשֶׁר בָּרָא.
בָּרוּךְ אַתָּה יהוה, הַזָּן אֶת הַכֹּל.

נוֹדֶה לְךָ יהוה אֱלֹהֵינוּ
עַל שֶׁהִנְחַלְתָּ לָנוּ וְלַאֲבוֹתֵינוּ
אֶרֶץ חֶמְדָּה טוֹבָה וּרְחָבָה
וְעַל שֶׁהוֹצֵאתָנוּ יהוה אֱלֹהֵינוּ מֵאֶרֶץ מִצְרַיִם
וּפְדִיתָנוּ מִבֵּית עֲבָדִים
וְעַל בְּרִיתְךָ שֶׁחָתַמְתָּ בִּבְשָׂרֵנוּ
וְעַל תּוֹרָתְךָ שֶׁלִּמַּדְתָּנוּ
וְעַל חֻקֶּיךָ שֶׁהוֹדַעְתָּנוּ
וְעַל חַיִּים חֵן וָחֶסֶד שֶׁחוֹנַנְתָּנוּ

sake of discharging the obligations, because if he were to eat them together, the biblical obligation to eat the matza would nullify the rabbinic commandment to eat the maror. This discussion implies that if the maror were to also be a biblical obligation, then the sages would at least accept that the matza and maror (without the Pesah) could be eaten together, because neither would nullify the other, but if he were to add the Pesah to his sandwich, two of the ingredients would combine to nullify another.

Shulhan Oreich

The participants continue with their holiday meal and may consume whatever they wish, and they should conclude the meal with at least an olive's volume of the meat of the Pesah.

If one has only the minimum amount of the Pesah's meat, he should save it for the conclusion of the meal, and recite the blessing, above, right before eating it.

After finishing his meal with the Korban Pesah, one should not eat or drink anything else that night except for the latter two cups of wine, and water. The sages also decreed that one should make sure to finish eating the Korban Pesah by midnight.

Bareich

The hands are washed, but no blessing is recited. The third cup of wine is filled, and the following Grace is recited thereon. Three or more men who ate together need to invite each other to say the Grace together, using the following formula, but every one of the participants should still have his own cup of wine.

The leader begins:

Gentlemen, let us recite the blessing

The other participants respond:

May the Name of the Lord be blessed from now and forever.

The Leader continues:

With the permission of our masters and superiors, let us bless [our God] of Whose we have eaten. Blessed is our God/He of Whose we have eaten and by Whose goodness we live. Blessed is our God/He of Whose we have eaten and by Whose goodness we live.

Tosefta P'sahim 2:15 says that Hillel the Elder would make a sandwich using all three critical foods: the Pesah, matza, and maror, and eat all of them at once, but in Yerushalmi Halla 1:1 Rabbi Johanan claims that Hillel's colleagues disagreed with Hillel, and that one should not do like Hillel did. In any event, when the Pesah is not present, the sages established that after one has fulfilled his obligations to eat both matza and maror, he should then eat some matza and maror together, in memory of the Temple, but that they should not be eaten in tandem for the

אוכלים ושותים בסעודה כל מה רוצים, ויסיימו באכילת לפחות מכזית הפסח.

ואם יש לו רק כזית אחד, ישמרהו עד הסוף כשהוא שבע, ויאכל אותו אז, ויברך הברכה "על אכילת הפסח" עובר לעשייתו.

ואינו טועם אחרי הכזית האחרון שום מאכל, חוץ משני הכוסות האחרונים. מתקנת חז״ל, חייבים לסיים את אכילת הפסח עד חצות הלילה.

נוטלים לידים בלי ברכה, ומוזגים כוס שלישי ומברכים ברכת המזון. שלשה שאכלו כאחד חייבים לזמן, אבל לכל המסובים יהיה כוס, והמזמן פותח:

רַבּוֹתַי נְבָרֵךְ:

המסבים עונים:

יְהִי שֵׁם יהוה מְבֹרָךְ מֵעַתָּה וְעַד עוֹלָם.

המזמן אומר:

**בִּרְשׁוּת מָרָנָן וְרַבָּנָן וְרַבּוֹתַי,
נְבָרֵךְ [אֱלֹהֵינוּ] שֶׁאָכַלְנוּ מִשֶּׁלּוֹ.**

המסבים עונים:

בָּרוּךְ [אֱלֹהֵינוּ] שֶׁאָכַלְנוּ מִשֶּׁלּוֹ וּבְטוּבוֹ חָיִינוּ.

המזמן חוזר ואומר:

בָּרוּךְ [אֱלֹהֵינוּ] שֶׁאָכַלְנוּ מִשֶּׁלּוֹ וּבְטוּבוֹ חָיִינוּ.

Hagiga

The hagiga offering of the fourteenth of Nisan is voluntarily, not obligatory, and its meat may (technically) be eaten already on the fourteenth, the entire night of the seder, and the following day, like any other peace offering.

When is a hagiga offering brought [with the Pesah]? When the Pesah is brought on a weekday, and in purity, and when the meat of the Pesah is scant. However, if the fourteenth of Nisan is the Sabbath, or if the Pesah is brought in impurity, or if there were more than enough Pesahim, A hagiga is not brought with it, and only the Pesah is offered.

If there is some meat of the hagiga at the seder, the following blessing is recited before its consumption:

Blessed are You, O Lord, our God, King of the Universe, Who has sanctified us with His commandments, and commanded us concerning the consumption of the sacrifice.

The hagiga's meat is then eaten.

Pesah

(One who has only an olive's volume of the Pesah should save it for consumption after his holiday meal.) The leader takes some of the Pesah's meat and recites the following blessing:

Blessed are You, O Lord, our God, King of the Universe, Who has sanctified us with His commandments, and commanded us concerning the consumption of the Pesah.

The Pesah meat is then eaten.

חֲגִיגָה

חגיגת ארבעה עשר רשות, ואינה חובה; והיא נאכלת לשני ימים ולילה אחד, ככל זבחי שלמים.

אֵימָתַי מְבִיאִין חֲגִיגָה עִם הַפֶּסַח?

בִּזְמַן שֶׁהוּא בָּא בַּחֹל וּבְטָהֳרָה וּבְמוּעָט.

אֲבָל אִם חָל יוֹם אַרְבָּעָה עָשָׂר לִהְיוֹת בַּשַּׁבָּת

אוֹ שֶׁבָּא הַפֶּסַח בְּטֻמְאָה

אוֹ שֶׁהָיוּ הַפְּסָחִים מְרֻבִּים

אֵין מְבִיאִין עִמּוֹ חֲגִיגָה

וְאֵין מַקְרִיבִין אֶלָּא הַפְּסָחִים בִּלְבָד.

אם יש שם בשר חגיגית ארבעה עשר יברך:

בָּרוּךְ אַתָּה יהוה, אֱלֹהֵינוּ מֶלֶךְ הָעוֹלָם אֲשֶׁר קִדְּשָׁנוּ בְּמִצְוֹתָיו וְצִוָּנוּ עַל אֲכִילַת הַזֶּבַח.

ואוכלו.

פֶּסַח

(מי שאין לו אלא כזית בשר לבד, ישמרהו לאחר הסעודה, וראה למטה.)
לוקח מבשר הפסח ומברך:

בָּרוּךְ אַתָּה יהוה, אֱלֹהֵינוּ מֶלֶךְ הָעוֹלָם אֲשֶׁר קִדְּשָׁנוּ בְּמִצְוֹתָיו וְצִוָּנוּ עַל אֲכִילַת הַפֶּסַח.

ואוכלו.

Motzi Matza

The leader takes the two matzot and breaks one of them. Holding the pieces with the whole matza, he recites the following two blessings:

Blessed are You, O Lord, our God, King of the Universe, Who brings forth bread from the earth.

Blessed are You, O Lord, our God, King of the Universe, Who has sanctified us with His commandments, and commanded us concerning the consumption of matza.

The matza is then eaten by the participants.

Maror

The leader takes some of the bitter herbs and dips them in the haroset. Then he recites the following blessing:

Blessed are You, O Lord, our God, King of the Universe, Who has sanctified us with His commandments, and commanded us concerning the consumption of maror.

The maror is then eaten by the participants.

According to Maimonides, one may choose to fulfill the commandments of eating matza and maror simultaneously by making a sandwich of the matza and maror. In such a case, the sandwich should be dipped in the haroset, and the following blessing, to be recited right before eating the sandwich, replaces the previous two blessings:

Blessed are You, O Lord, our God, King of the Universe, Who has sanctified us with His commandments, and commanded us concerning the consumption of matza and maror.

The sandwich is then eaten.

מוֹצִיא מַצָּה

יקח שתי המצות, ויפרוס אחת מהן. יניח הפרוסה בתוך השלמה ויברך שתי ברכות:

בָּרוּךְ אַתָּה יהוה, אֱלֹהֵינוּ מֶלֶךְ הָעוֹלָם הַמּוֹצִיא לֶחֶם מִן הָאָרֶץ.

בָּרוּךְ אַתָּה יהוה, אֱלֹהֵינוּ מֶלֶךְ הָעוֹלָם אֲשֶׁר קִדְּשָׁנוּ בְּמִצְוֹתָיו וְצִוָּנוּ עַל אֲכִילַת מַצָּה.

ואוכל את המצה.

מָרוֹר

יקח את המרור ויטבלו בחרוסת ויברך:

בָּרוּךְ אַתָּה יהוה, אֱלֹהֵינוּ מֶלֶךְ הָעוֹלָם אֲשֶׁר קִדְּשָׁנוּ בְּמִצְוֹתָיו וְצִוָּנוּ עַל אֲכִילַת מָרוֹר.

ואוכל את המרור.

לשיטת הרמב"ם, יכול לכרוך מצה ומרור ולטבלם בחרוסת ולאכלם בבת אחת, ובמקום שתי הברכות דלעיל, יברך ברכה זו לפני האכילה:

בָּרוּךְ אַתָּה יהוה, אֱלֹהֵינוּ מֶלֶךְ הָעוֹלָם אֲשֶׁר קִדְּשָׁנוּ בְּמִצְוֹתָיו וְצִוָּנוּ עַל אֲכִילַת מַצָּה וּמְרוֹרִים.

ואוכל את כריך המצה והמרור.

The cups of wine are lifted and the following two blessings are recited.

**Blessed are you O Lord, our God,
King of the universe,
Who has redeemed us
and Who redeemed our ancestors from Egypt,
and brought us to this night
to eat the Pesah, matza, and maror thereon
rejoicing in Your city and exulting in Your service,
and we thank You
for our redemption and our personal deliverance.
Blessed are You, O Lord,
Who has redeemed Israel.**

According to some authorities, this latter blessing is omitted:

**Blessed are You, O Lord, our God, King of the universe,
Creator of the fruit of the vine.**

The second cup is then drunk.

> rejoicing in the building of Your city and exulting in Your service, and there we shall eat of the sacrifices and from the Passover offerings whose blood shall reach the wall of Your altar in favor, and we shall thank You… The text of this blessing has been updated to reflect the new, more fortunate reality.

Rohtza

The hands are ritually washed in preparation for eating the matza,
and the following blessing is recited:

**Blessed are You, O Lord, our God, King of the Universe,
Who has sanctified us with His commandments,
and commanded us
concerning the ritual washing of the hands.**

מגביהים את הכוסות ומברכים שתי ברכות:

בָּרוּךְ אַתָּה יהוה, אֱלֹהֵינוּ מֶלֶךְ הָעוֹלָם
אֲשֶׁר גְּאָלָנוּ וְגָאַל אֶת אֲבוֹתֵינוּ מִמִּצְרַיִם
וְהִגִּיעָנוּ לַלַּיְלָה הַזֶּה
לֶאֱכָל־בּוֹ פֶּסַח מַצָּה וּמָרוֹר
שְׂמֵחִים בְּעִירְךָ וְשָׂשִׂים בַּעֲבוֹדָתֶךָ
וּמוֹדִים אֲנַחְנוּ לָךְ
עַל גְּאֻלָּתֵנוּ וְעַל פְּדוּת נַפְשֵׁנוּ.
בָּרוּךְ אַתָּה יהוה, גָּאַל יִשְׂרָאֵל.

מנהג האשכנזים לברך ברכה זו, ומנהג הבית יוסף שאין לברך:

בָּרוּךְ אַתָּה יהוה, אֱלֹהֵינוּ מֶלֶךְ הָעוֹלָם
בּוֹרֵא פְּרִי הַגָּפֶן.

ושותים את הכוס בהסבת שמאל.

When the seder was conducted without the Korban Pesah, the previous blessing had an additional prayer that the celebrants merit to participate in a seder which features the Korban Pesah: So too, O Lord, our God and God of our ancestors, bring us to other appointed times and holidays that will come upon us in peace,

נוטלים את הידים ומברכים:

בָּרוּךְ אַתָּה יהוה, אֱלֹהֵינוּ מֶלֶךְ הָעוֹלָם
אֲשֶׁר קִדְּשָׁנוּ בְּמִצְוֹתָיו, וְצִוָּנוּ עַל נְטִילַת יָדָיִם.

Hallelujah!
Praise, you servants of the Lord
                              praise the name of the Lord.
Blessed be the name of the Lord   from now and forever.
From the rising of the sun until its setting
                              the Lord's name is praised.
The Lord is lofty above all nations
                              His glory is upon the heavens.
Who is like the Lord our God Who is enthroned on high,
Who looks downward   upon heaven and the earth?
Who raises up the poor from the dust?
                        Who lifts the destitute from the trash heaps
To seat him among dignitaries
                            with dignitaries of his people.
Who seats the barren woman in the house
                            as a joyful mother of children.
Hallelujah!

When Israel came out of Egypt
           the house of Jacob from a people of alien tongue,
Judah was His Sanctuary   Israel, His dominion.
The sea saw, and fled   the Jordan turned backward.
The mountains skipped like rams
                            the hills like young sheep.
What is with you, O sea, that you flee?
                        O Jordan, that you turn backward?
O mountains, that you skip like rams
                            hills, like young sheep?
In the presence of the Master, tremble, O earth
                        in the presence of the God of Jacob
Who turns the rock into a pool of water
                        the flint into a fountain of waters.

מַגִּיד

הַלְלוּיָהּ!
הַלְלוּ עַבְדֵי יהוה   הַלְלוּ אֶת שֵׁם יהוה.
יְהִי שֵׁם יהוה מְבֹרָךְ   מֵעַתָּה וְעַד עוֹלָם.
מִמִּזְרַח שֶׁמֶשׁ עַד מְבוֹאוֹ   מְהֻלָּל שֵׁם יהוה.
רָם עַל כָּל גּוֹיִם יהוה   עַל הַשָּׁמַיִם כְּבוֹדוֹ.
מִי כַּיהוה אֱלֹהֵינוּ   הַמַּגְבִּיהִי לָשָׁבֶת.
הַמַּשְׁפִּילִי לִרְאוֹת   בַּשָּׁמַיִם וּבָאָרֶץ.
מְקִימִי מֵעָפָר דָּל   מֵאַשְׁפֹּת יָרִים אֶבְיוֹן.
לְהוֹשִׁיבִי עִם נְדִיבִים   עִם נְדִיבֵי עַמּוֹ.
מוֹשִׁיבִי עֲקֶרֶת הַבַּיִת   אֵם הַבָּנִים שְׂמֵחָה.
הַלְלוּיָהּ!

בְּצֵאת יִשְׂרָאֵל מִמִּצְרָיִם   בֵּית יַעֲקֹב מֵעַם לֹעֵז.
הָיְתָה יְהוּדָה לְקָדְשׁוֹ   יִשְׂרָאֵל מַמְשְׁלוֹתָיו.
הַיָּם רָאָה וַיָּנֹס   הַיַּרְדֵּן יִסֹּב לְאָחוֹר.
הֶהָרִים רָקְדוּ כְאֵילִים   גְּבָעוֹת כִּבְנֵי צֹאן.
מַה לְּךָ הַיָּם כִּי תָנוּס   הַיַּרְדֵּן תִּסֹּב לְאָחוֹר.
הֶהָרִים תִּרְקְדוּ כְאֵילִים   גְּבָעוֹת כִּבְנֵי צֹאן.
מִלִּפְנֵי אָדוֹן חוּלִי אָרֶץ   מִלִּפְנֵי אֱלוֹהַּ יַעֲקֹב.
הַהֹפְכִי הַצּוּר אֲגַם מָיִם   חַלָּמִישׁ לְמַעְיְנוֹ מָיִם.

with mortar and bricks,
and in all manner of work in the field,
in all of their work which was backbreaking.

In every generation, one is obligated to view himself
as if he himself has left Egypt, as it is said,
"On that day, you shall tell your son, saying:
for the sake of this, did the Lord do this for me
when I left Egypt."
Not only did the Holy One, Blessed is He,
redeem our ancestors.
Rather, He also redeemed us along with them,
as it is said, He took us out from there
in order to bring us,
to give us the land which He swore to our fathers.

<small>The leader holds the cup in his hand and says:</small>

**Therefore, we are obligated to thank,
praise, laud, glorify, exalt,
lavish, bless, elevate, and acclaim
He who wrought all these miracles
for our ancestors and for us.
He took us out from slavery to freedom,
from sorrow to happiness,
from mourning to celebration,
from darkness to great light,
and from servitude to redemption.
Thus, let us say a new song before Him.
Hallelujah!**

בְּחֹמֶר וּבִלְבֵנִים וּבְכָל עֲבֹדָה בַּשָּׂדֶה
אֵת כָּל עֲבֹדָתָם אֲשֶׁר עָבְדוּ בָהֶם בְּפָרֶךְ.

בְּכָל־דּוֹר וָדוֹר חַיָּב אָדָם לִרְאוֹת אֶת עַצְמוֹ
כְּאִלּוּ הוּא יָצָא מִמִּצְרַיִם, שֶׁנֶּאֱמַר:
וְהִגַּדְתָּ לְבִנְךָ בַּיּוֹם הַהוּא לֵאמֹר

מגיד

בַּעֲבוּר זֶה עָשָׂה יהוה לִי בְּצֵאתִי מִמִּצְרָיִם.
לֹא אֶת אֲבוֹתֵינוּ בִּלְבַד גָּאַל הַקָּדוֹשׁ בָּרוּךְ הוּא
אֶלָּא אַף אוֹתָנוּ גָּאַל עִמָּהֶם
שֶׁנֶּאֱמַר: וְאוֹתָנוּ הוֹצִיא מִשָּׁם
לְמַעַן הָבִיא אֹתָנוּ
לָתֶת לָנוּ אֶת הָאָרֶץ אֲשֶׁר נִשְׁבַּע לַאֲבֹתֵנוּ.

יאחז הכוס בידו ויאמר:

לְפִיכָךְ אֲנַחְנוּ חַיָּבִים לְהוֹדוֹת
לְהַלֵּל, לְשַׁבֵּחַ, לְפָאֵר, לְרוֹמֵם
לְהַדֵּר, לְבָרֵךְ, לְעַלֵּה, וּלְקַלֵּס
לְמִי שֶׁעָשָׂה לַאֲבוֹתֵינוּ וְלָנוּ אֶת כָּל הַנִּסִּים הָאֵלּוּ.
הוֹצִיאָנוּ מֵעַבְדוּת לְחֵרוּת
מִיָּגוֹן לְשִׂמְחָה, וּמֵאֵבֶל לְיוֹם טוֹב
וּמֵאֲפֵלָה לְאוֹר גָּדוֹל, וּמִשִּׁעְבּוּד לִגְאֻלָּה.
וְנֹאמַר לְפָנָיו שִׁירָה חֲדָשָׁה.
הַלְלוּיָהּ!

The leader points to the meat of the Pesah and says:

This Pesah that we eat, in perpetuation of what?
In perpetuation of when the Holy One, blessed is He,
passed over the houses of our ancestors in Egypt,
as it is said, "You shall say:
It is the Lord's Passover sacrifice,
that He passed over
the houses of the children of Israel in Egypt
when He smote the Egyptians and saved our houses.
Then the people bowed and prostrated themselves."

The leader holds the matza in his hand and shows it to the others, and says.

This matza that we eat, in perpetuation of what?
In perpetuation of our ancestors' dough
not having the time to rise
before the King of kings, the Holy One, blessed is He,
appeared to them and redeemed them,
as it is said, they baked the dough
that they had brought out of Egypt,
into loaves of matza for it was not leavened,
because they were driven out of Egypt
and could not tarry,
and they had not made provisions for themselves.

The leader shows the maror to the others and says:

These bitter herbs that we eat,
in perpetuation of what?
In perpetuation of the Egyptians' embittering the
lives of our ancestors in Egypt,
as it is said,
they embittered their lives with hard work,

מצביע על קרבן הפסח ואומר:

פֶּסַח זֶה שֶׁאָנוּ אוֹכְלִים, עַל שׁוּם מָה?

עַל שׁוּם שֶׁפָּסַח הַקָּדוֹשׁ בָּרוּךְ הוּא
עַל בָּתֵּי אֲבוֹתֵינוּ בְּמִצְרַיִם
שֶׁנֶּאֱמַר: וַאֲמַרְתֶּם זֶבַח פֶּסַח הוּא לַיהוה
אֲשֶׁר פָּסַח עַל בָּתֵּי בְּנֵי יִשְׂרָאֵל בְּמִצְרַיִם
בְּנָגְפּוֹ אֶת מִצְרַיִם וְאֶת בָּתֵּינוּ הִצִּיל.
וַיִּקֹּד הָעָם וַיִּשְׁתַּחֲוּוּ.

מגיד

אוחז המצה בידו ומראה אותה למסובין:

מַצָּה זוֹ שֶׁאָנוּ אוֹכְלִים, עַל שׁוּם מָה?

עַל שׁוּם שֶׁלֹּא הִסְפִּיק בְּצֵקָם שֶׁל אֲבוֹתֵינוּ לְהַחֲמִיץ
עַד שֶׁנִּגְלָה עֲלֵיהֶם מֶלֶךְ מַלְכֵי הַמְּלָכִים
הַקָּדוֹשׁ בָּרוּךְ הוּא, וּגְאָלָם, שֶׁנֶּאֱמַר:
וַיֹּאפוּ אֶת הַבָּצֵק אֲשֶׁר הוֹצִיאוּ מִמִּצְרַיִם
עֻגֹת מַצּוֹת כִּי לֹא חָמֵץ
כִּי גֹרְשׁוּ מִמִּצְרַיִם וְלֹא יָכְלוּ לְהִתְמַהְמֵהַּ
וְגַם צֵדָה לֹא עָשׂוּ לָהֶם.

אוחז המרור בידו ומראה אותו למסובין:

מָרוֹר זֶה שֶׁאָנוּ אוֹכְלִים, עַל שׁוּם מָה?

עַל שׁוּם שֶׁמֵּרְרוּ הַמִּצְרִים אֶת חַיֵּי אֲבוֹתֵינוּ בְּמִצְרַיִם
שֶׁנֶּאֱמַר: וַיְמָרְרוּ אֶת חַיֵּיהֶם בַּעֲבֹדָה קָשָׁה

supplied our needs in the wilderness for forty years,
fed us the manna,
gave us the Sabbath,
drew us to Mount Sinai,
gave us the Torah,
brought us into the land of Israel,
and built the chosen Temple for us
in order to atone for all of our sins.

The tray with the bitter herbs, the matzot, and the sacrificial meat(s) is brought back to the leader.

Rabban Gamliel used to say,
Anyone who has not made mention
of these three things on Passover
has not discharged his obligation,
and they are:

the Pesah, matza, and bitter herbs.

וְסִפֵּק צָרְכֵּנוּ בַּמִּדְבָּר אַרְבָּעִים שָׁנָה
וְהֶאֱכִילָנוּ אֶת הַמָּן
וְנָתַן לָנוּ אֶת הַשַּׁבָּת
וְקֵרְבָנוּ לִפְנֵי הַר סִינַי
וְנָתַן לָנוּ אֶת הַתּוֹרָה
וְהִכְנִיסָנוּ לְאֶרֶץ יִשְׂרָאֵל
וּבָנָה לָנוּ אֶת בֵּית הַבְּחִירָה
לְכַפֵּר עַל כָּל־עֲוֹנוֹתֵינוּ.

מגיד

מחזירים את המגש עם המרור, המצות, ובשר הקרבנות.

רַבָּן גַּמְלִיאֵל הָיָה אוֹמֵר:
כָּל שֶׁלֹּא אָמַר שְׁלֹשָׁה דְבָרִים אֵלּוּ בְּפֶסַח
לֹא יָצָא יְדֵי חוֹבָתוֹ
וְאֵלּוּ הֵן:

פֶּסַח, מַצָּה, וּמָרוֹר.

If He had given us the Sabbath,
but had not brought us close to Mount Sinai,
it would have been enough for us.

If He had brought us close to Mount Sinai,
but had not given us the Torah,
it would have been enough for us.

If He had given us the Torah,
but had not brought us into the land of Israel,
it would have been enough for us.

If He had brought us into the land of Israel,
but had not built the chosen Temple for us,
it would have been enough for us.

How much more so has the double-
and four-fold favor of the Omnipresent
been good for us:
He took us out of Egypt,
meted out justice among them
and among their gods,
killed their firstborn,
gave us their money,
split the sea for us
and brought us through it on dry land,
sank our enemies in the sea,

מגיד

אִלּוּ נָתַן לָנוּ אֶת הַשַּׁבָּת
וְלֹא קֵרְבָנוּ לִפְנֵי הַר סִינַי, דַּיֵּנוּ.

אִלּוּ קֵרְבָנוּ לִפְנֵי הַר סִינַי
וְלֹא נָתַן לָנוּ אֶת הַתּוֹרָה, דַּיֵּנוּ.

אִלּוּ נָתַן לָנוּ אֶת הַתּוֹרָה
וְלֹא הִכְנִיסָנוּ לְאֶרֶץ יִשְׂרָאֵל, דַּיֵּנוּ.

אִלּוּ הִכְנִיסָנוּ לְאֶרֶץ יִשְׂרָאֵל
וְלֹא בָנָה לָנוּ אֶת בֵּית הַבְּחִירָה, דַּיֵּנוּ.

עַל אַחַת, כַּמָּה וְכַמָּה
טוֹבָה כְפוּלָה וּמְכֻפֶּלֶת לַמָּקוֹם עָלֵינוּ:
שֶׁהוֹצִיאָנוּ מִמִּצְרַיִם
וְעָשָׂה בָהֶם שְׁפָטִים
וְעָשָׂה בֵאלֹהֵיהֶם
וְהָרַג אֶת בְּכוֹרֵיהֶם
וְנָתַן לָנוּ אֶת מָמוֹנָם
וְקָרַע לָנוּ אֶת הַיָּם
וְהֶעֱבִירָנוּ בְּתוֹכוֹ בֶּחָרָבָה
וְשִׁקַּע צָרֵנוּ בְּתוֹכוֹ

If He had meted out justice to their gods,
but had not killed their firstborn,
it would have been enough for us.

If He had killed their firstborn,
but had not given us their money,
it would have been enough for us.

If He had given us their money,
but had not split the Sea for us,
it would have been enough for us.

If He had split the Sea for us,
but had not taken us through it on dry land,
it would have been enough for us.

If He had taken us through it on dry land,
but had not sunk our enemies in the sea,
it would have been enough for us.

If He had sunk our enemies in the sea,
but had not supplied our needs in the wilderness for
forty years, it would have been enough for us.

If He had supplied our needs in the wilderness for
forty years, but had not fed us the manna,
it would have been enough for us.

If He had fed us the manna,
but had not given us the Sabbath,
it would have been enough for us.

אִלּוּ עָשָׂה בֵאלֹהֵיהֶם
וְלֹא הָרַג אֶת בְּכוֹרֵיהֶם, דַּיֵּינוּ.

אִלּוּ הָרַג אֶת בְּכוֹרֵיהֶם
וְלֹא נָתַן לָנוּ אֶת מָמוֹנָם, דַּיֵּינוּ.

מגיד

אִלּוּ נָתַן לָנוּ אֶת מָמוֹנָם
וְלֹא קָרַע לָנוּ אֶת הַיָּם, דַּיֵּינוּ.

אִלּוּ קָרַע לָנוּ אֶת הַיָּם
וְלֹא הֶעֱבִירָנוּ בְּתוֹכוֹ בֶּחָרָבָה, דַּיֵּינוּ.

אִלּוּ הֶעֱבִירָנוּ בְּתוֹכוֹ בֶּחָרָבָה
וְלֹא שִׁקַּע צָרֵנוּ בְּתוֹכוֹ, דַּיֵּינוּ.

אִלּוּ שִׁקַּע צָרֵנוּ בְּתוֹכוֹ
וְלֹא סִפֵּק צָרְכֵּנוּ בַּמִּדְבָּר אַרְבָּעִים שָׁנָה, דַּיֵּינוּ.

אִלּוּ סִפֵּק צָרְכֵּנוּ בַּמִּדְבָּר אַרְבָּעִים שָׁנָה
וְלֹא הֶאֱכִילָנוּ אֶת הַמָּן, דַּיֵּינוּ.

אִלּוּ הֶאֱכִילָנוּ אֶת הַמָּן
וְלֹא נָתַן לָנוּ אֶת הַשַּׁבָּת, דַּיֵּינוּ.

"And He brought us to this place,
and He gave us this land,
a land flowing with milk and honey."

He brought us to this place –
This refers to the Holy Temple.
Maybe it refers to the land of Israel?
When it then says, "and He gave us this land,"
that is a reference to the land of Israel.
What does it mean to teach us by adding
"And He brought us to this place?"
In reward for our coming to this place,
He gave us this land,
a land flowing with milk and honey.

> strengthens the claim that Israel inherits the land in the merit of conducting the sacrificial ritual.

The Omnipresent has done so much good for us!

**If He had taken us out of Egypt,
but not meted out justice to them,
it would have been enough for us.**

**If He had meted out justice to them,
but not to their gods,
it would have been enough for us.**

וַיְבִאֵנוּ אֶל הַמָּקוֹם הַזֶּה
וַיִּתֶּן לָנוּ אֶת הָאָרֶץ הַזֹּאת
אֶרֶץ זָבַת חָלָב וּדְבָשׁ.

וַיְבִאֵנוּ אֶל הַמָּקוֹם הַזֶּה.
זֶה בֵּית הַמִּקְדָּשׁ.
אוֹ יָכוֹל זֶה אֶרֶץ יִשְׂרָאֵל?
כְּשֶׁהוּא אוֹמֵר וַיִּתֶּן לָנוּ אֶת הָאָרֶץ הַזֹּאת
הֲוֵי אוֹמֵר זוֹ אֶרֶץ יִשְׂרָאֵל.
וּמַה תַּלְמוּד לוֹמַר וַיְבִאֵנוּ אֶל הַמָּקוֹם הַזֶּה?
בִּשְׂכַר בִּיאָתֵנוּ אֶל הַמָּקוֹם הַזֶּה
נָתַן לָנוּ אֶת הָאָרֶץ הַזֹּאת
אֶרֶץ זָבַת חָלָב וּדְבָשׁ.

מגיד

This section appears in the Sifre to Parashat Ki Tavo as the continuation of the exposition of the previous verses that forms the majority of Maggid. This

כַּמָּה מַעֲלוֹת טוֹבוֹת לַמָּקוֹם עָלֵינוּ!

אִלּוּ הוֹצִיאָנוּ מִמִּצְרַיִם
וְלֹא עָשָׂה בָהֶם שְׁפָטִים, דַּיֵּנוּ.

אִלּוּ עָשָׂה בָהֶם שְׁפָטִים
וְלֹא עָשָׂה בֵאלֹהֵיהֶם, דַּיֵּנוּ.

wrath, and fury, and trouble;
a band of destructive angels."
Wrath is one,
and fury is two,
and trouble is three,
a band of destructive angels is four.

You may conclude from this
that in Egypt they were struck with forty plagues,
while at the sea
they were struck with two hundred plagues.

Rabbi Akiva says,
How can it be known that every plague
that the Holy One, blessed is He,
brought upon the Egyptians in Egypt
was actually five plagues?
For it is said,
"He sent upon them the fierceness of His anger,
wrath, and fury, and trouble;
a band of destructive angels."
The fierceness of His anger is one,
Wrath is two,
and fury is three,
and trouble is four,
a band of destructive angels is five.
You may conclude from this
that in Egypt they were struck with fifty plagues,
while at the sea
they were struck with two hundred and fifty plagues.

עֶבְרָה וָזַעַם וְצָרָה מִשְׁלַחַת מַלְאֲכֵי רָעִים.

עֶבְרָה - אַחַת

וָזַעַם - שְׁתַּיִם

וְצָרָה - שָׁלֹשׁ

מִשְׁלַחַת מַלְאֲכֵי רָעִים - אַרְבַּע.

אֱמֹר מֵעַתָּה: בְּמִצְרַיִם לָקוּ אַרְבָּעִים מַכּוֹת וְעַל הַיָּם לָקוּ מָאתַיִם מַכּוֹת.

רַבִּי עֲקִיבָא אוֹמֵר:

מִנַּיִן שֶׁכָּל מַכָּה וּמַכָּה שֶׁהֵבִיא הַקָּדוֹשׁ בָּרוּךְ הוּא עַל הַמִּצְרִים בְּמִצְרַיִם הָיְתָה שֶׁל חָמֵשׁ מַכּוֹת?

שֶׁנֶּאֱמַר: יְשַׁלַּח בָּם חֲרוֹן אַפּוֹ עֶבְרָה וָזַעַם וְצָרָה מִשְׁלַחַת מַלְאֲכֵי רָעִים.

חֲרוֹן אַפּוֹ - אַחַת

עֶבְרָה - שְׁתַּיִם

וָזַעַם - שָׁלֹשׁ

וְצָרָה - אַרְבַּע

מִשְׁלַחַת מַלְאֲכֵי רָעִים - חָמֵשׁ.

אֱמֹר מֵעַתָּה: בְּמִצְרַיִם לָקוּ חֲמִשִּׁים מַכּוֹת וְעַל הַיָּם לָקוּ חֲמִשִּׁים וּמָאתַיִם מַכּוֹת.

Rabbi Jose the Galilean says
How do you know
that the Egyptians were struck
with ten plagues in Egypt
and with fifty plagues at the sea?
Regarding Egypt, what does it say?
The sorcerers said to Pharaoh,
"This is God's finger."
Regarding the sea, what does it say?
"Israel saw the great hand
which the Lord used against Egypt,
and the people feared the Lord;
they believed in the Lord and His servant Moses."
How many did they suffer from the finger?
Ten plagues.

You may conclude from this that in Egypt,
they were struck with ten plagues,
while at the sea, they were struck with fifty plagues.

Rabbi Eliezer says,
How can it be known that every plague
that the Holy One, blessed is He,
brought upon the Egyptians in Egypt
was actually four plagues?
For it is said,
"He sent upon them the fierceness of His anger:

רַבִּי יוֹסֵי הַגְּלִילִי אוֹמֵר:
מִנַּיִן אַתָּה אוֹמֵר
שֶׁלָּקוּ הַמִּצְרִים בְּמִצְרַיִם עֶשֶׂר מַכּוֹת
וְעַל הַיָּם לָקוּ חֲמִשִּׁים מַכּוֹת?
בְּמִצְרַיִם מָה הוּא אוֹמֵר?
וַיֹּאמְרוּ הַחַרְטֻמִּים אֶל פַּרְעֹה
אֶצְבַּע אֱלֹהִים הִוא.
וְעַל הַיָּם מָה הוּא אוֹמֵר?
וַיַּרְא יִשְׂרָאֵל אֶת הַיָּד הַגְּדֹלָה
אֲשֶׁר עָשָׂה יהוה בְּמִצְרַיִם
וַיִּירְאוּ הָעָם אֶת יהוה
וַיַּאֲמִינוּ בַּיהוה וּבְמֹשֶׁה עַבְדּוֹ.
כַּמָּה לָקוּ בְאֶצְבַּע? עֶשֶׂר מַכּוֹת.

אֱמֹר מֵעַתָּה: בְּמִצְרַיִם לָקוּ עֶשֶׂר מַכּוֹת
וְעַל הַיָּם לָקוּ חֲמִשִּׁים מַכּוֹת.

רַבִּי אֱלִיעֶזֶר אוֹמֵר:
מִנַּיִן שֶׁכָּל מַכָּה וּמַכָּה שֶׁהֵבִיא הַקָּדוֹשׁ בָּרוּךְ הוּא
עַל הַמִּצְרִים בְּמִצְרַיִם
הָיְתָה שֶׁל אַרְבַּע מַכּוֹת?
שֶׁנֶּאֱמַר: יְשַׁלַּח בָּם חֲרוֹן אַפּוֹ

Blood
Frogs
Lice
Wild Animals
Pestilence
Boils
Hail
Locusts
Darkness
Death of the Firstborn

Rabbi Judah arranged them by their initials:

D'tzach 'Addash B'ahav.

מגיד

דָּם
צְפַרְדֵּעַ
כִּנִּים
עָרוֹב
דֶּבֶר
שְׁחִין
בָּרָד
אַרְבֶּה
חֹשֶׁךְ
מַכַּת בְּכוֹרוֹת.

רַבִּי יְהוּדָה הָיָה נוֹתֵן בָּהֶם סִמָּנִים:

דְּצַ"ךְ עֲדַ"שׁ בְּאַחַ"ב.

blood, and fire, and mushroom clouds."

Maggid

lit., do not allow it to leaven, that is, do not miss it. 2. The punctilious perform commandments as soon as possible. 3. The priests (when officiating) are punctilious. These principles teach us that punctiliousness in the divine service is a virtue, while procrastination is a vice, and therefore, it is proper to offer sacrifice only from that which is done with alacrity, and not from that which has been delayed.

Moses blessed the priestly tribe of Levi by saying, "they shall teach Your laws to Jacob and Your Torah to Israel; they shall place incense in Your presence, and a wholly burnt offering on Your altar." That is, how do the priests go about teaching the laws and Torah to Jacob and Israel? Through the service they perform on the altars. We learn how to perform the commandments by emulating the actions of the priests, and just as the meal offerings consumed on the altar and by the mouths of the priests are unleavened, so too, on Passover we only consume unleavened bread.

Alternatively,
With a mighty hand – is two,
with an outstretched arm – is two,
and with great awe – is two,
and with signs – is two,
and with wonders – is two.
These are ten plagues
that the Holy One, blessed is He,
brought upon the Egyptians in Egypt,
and they are:

Regarding leaven, we have seen two types of prohibitions, the general prohibitions against possessing leaven or allowing it to remain in our domains during the Passover festival, and the prohibition against possessing leaven when offering the Korban Pesah, during what we know as the afternoon of Passover Eve.

It is interesting to note that it is always forbidden to offer leaven on the Temple's altar, and that throughout the year, the meal offerings that are eaten by the priests, with the exception of the two loaves offered by the community on Pentecost, are unleavened. Passover, when the entire Jewish people is bidden to eat only unleavened bread, is once again a chance for the people to behave as the priests do within the Temple.

But why does the Torah generally prohibit leavened meal offerings? The answer, I believe, comes from the consideration of three principles enunciated by our sages: 1. If the opportunity to perform a commandment presents itself, *al tahmitzenna*,

דָּבָר אַחֵר:
בְּיָד חֲזָקָה - שְׁתַּיִם
וּבִזְרֹעַ נְטוּיָה - שְׁתַּיִם
וּבְמֹרָא גָּדֹל - שְׁתַּיִם
וּבְאֹתוֹת - שְׁתַּיִם
וּבְמֹפְתִים - שְׁתַּיִם.
אֵלּוּ עֶשֶׂר מַכּוֹת שֶׁהֵבִיא הַקָּדוֹשׁ בָּרוּךְ הוּא
עַל הַמִּצְרִים בְּמִצְרַיִם
וְאֵלּוּ הֵן:

With a mighty hand – this is the pestilence,
as it is said,
"Behold, the hand of the Lord
is upon your cattle which are in the field,
upon the horses, the donkeys, the camels,
the herds, and the flocks:
a very severe pestilence."

With an outstretched arm – this is the sword,
as it is said,
"And his sword drawn in his hand, set over Jerusalem."

And with great awe –
this is the revelation of the Divine Presence,
as it is said,
"Or has God ever tried to go to take for Himself
a nation from the midst of a nation,
through trials, signs, and wonders, and by war,
and by a mighty hand, an outstretched arm,
and great terrors
like the Lord your God did for you in Egypt
before your eyes?"

And with signs – this is the staff, as it is said,
"And take this staff in your hand;
you will perform the signs with it."

And wonders – this is the blood, as it is said,
"I will place wonders in the heavens and the earth:

מגיד

בְּיָד חֲזָקָה - זוֹ הַדֶּבֶר, כְּמָה שֶׁנֶּאֱמַר:
הִנֵּה יַד יהוה הוֹיָה בְּמִקְנְךָ אֲשֶׁר בַּשָּׂדֶה
בַּסּוּסִים, בַּחֲמֹרִים, בַּגְּמַלִּים, בַּבָּקָר, וּבַצֹּאן
דֶּבֶר כָּבֵד מְאֹד.

וּבִזְרֹעַ נְטוּיָה - זוֹ הַחֶרֶב כְּמָה שֶׁנֶּאֱמַר:
וְחַרְבּוֹ שְׁלוּפָה בְּיָדוֹ
נְטוּיָה עַל יְרוּשָׁלָיִם.

וּבְמוֹרָא גָּדֹל - זוֹ גִּלּוּי שְׁכִינָה.
כְּמָה שֶׁנֶּאֱמַר:
אוֹ הֲנִסָּה אֱלֹהִים לָבֹא לָקַחַת לוֹ גוֹי מִקֶּרֶב גּוֹי
בְּמַסֹּת בְּאֹתֹת וּבְמוֹפְתִים וּבְמִלְחָמָה
וּבְיָד חֲזָקָה וּבִזְרוֹעַ נְטוּיָה וּבְמוֹרָאִים גְּדֹלִים
כְּכֹל אֲשֶׁר עָשָׂה לָכֶם יהוה אֱלֹהֵיכֶם בְּמִצְרַיִם לְעֵינֶיךָ.

וּבְאֹתוֹת - זֶה הַמַּטֶּה, כְּמָה שֶׁנֶּאֱמַר:
וְאֶת הַמַּטֶּה הַזֶּה תִּקַּח בְּיָדֶךָ
אֲשֶׁר תַּעֲשֶׂה בּוֹ אֶת הָאֹתֹת.

וּבְמוֹפְתִים - זֶה הַדָּם, כְּמָה שֶׁנֶּאֱמַר:
וְנָתַתִּי מוֹפְתִים בַּשָּׁמַיִם וּבָאָרֶץ

sacrifice while leaven still exists, and the slaughter of the Passover sacrifice is on the fourteenth after noon. What is this riddance referred to by the Torah? One should nullify the leaven within his mind and to consider it as dust, and resolve that he has absolutely no leaven in his possession, and that whatever leaven he may have in his possession is like dust and a thing of no use whatsoever.

There are many more verses which link the slaughter of the Pesah with the prohibitions against leaven and the obligation to get rid of it. It is only in a later chapter that Maimonides explains how the leaven is to be destroyed: by burning it, by crumbling it and throwing it to the wind, and throwing it into the sea. The section above, which describes one's required mindset regarding the leaven, is reminiscent of his formulation regarding idolatry, which is essentially an intellectual sin in that the idolater believes that there are forces other than the True God that control this world. It seems from his writings that getting rid of the leaven is analogous to the repudiation of idolatry, both of which have to be removed from the mind. This explains why on Pesah Sheini, there are no commandments or prohibitions regarding the leaven, because it is not the anniversary of "the day after the Passover," "when the Egyptians were burying all the firstborn among them whom the Lord had smitten, and among their gods He meted out justice."

"I will pass through the Land of Egypt" –

I, and not an angel.

"And I will smite every firstborn in the land of Egypt"–

I, and not a seraph.

"And I will mete out justice to all the gods of Egypt"–

I, and not an agent.

"I am the Lord" –

I am Him, and not another.

Maimonides held that there are six biblical commandments regarding leaven on Passover:

a. the prohibition against eating leaven from noon of the fourteenth of Nisan onward, b. the commandment to get rid of all leaven from the fourteenth of Nisan, c. the prohibition against eating leaven all seven days, d. the prohibition against eating mixtures containing leaven all seven days, e. the prohibition against leaven being seen all seven days, and f. the prohibition against leaven being found all seven days. Note that the first and third of these commandments are considered separate: one is against eating leaven on the afternoon of the fourteenth of Nisan, while the other is the prohibition for the subsequent seven days, and that despite the prohibitions against seeing and finding leaven throughout Passover, there is also a positive commandment to get rid of the leaven, that is, to destroy it, on the day that the Passover sacrifice is offered. In Maimonides's words:

It is a positive commandment of the Torah to get rid of the leaven before the time when it is forbidden for consumption, as it is said, "On the first day, get rid of the sourdough from your homes." According to the oral tradition, "the first day" refers to the fourteenth of Nisan. Proof for this is written in the Torah: "Do not slaughter the blood of My sacrifice upon leaven." That is, do not slaughter the Passover

וְעָבַרְתִּי בְאֶרֶץ מִצְרַיִם בַּלַּיְלָה הַזֶּה
אֲנִי וְלֹא מַלְאָךְ.

וְהִכֵּיתִי כָל בְּכוֹר בְּאֶרֶץ מִצְרַיִם
אֲנִי וְלֹא שָׂרָף.

וּבְכָל אֱלֹהֵי מִצְרַיִם אֶעֱשֶׂה שְׁפָטִים
אֲנִי וְלֹא שָׁלִיחַ.

אֲנִי יהוה
אֲנִי הוּא, וְלֹא אַחֵר.

Our toil – this refers to the sons,
as it is said,
"Every son that is born you shall cast into the river,
and every daughter you shall keep alive."

And our oppression – this refers to the pressure,
as it is said, "I have also seen the pressure
which the Egyptians apply to them."

"The Lord took us out of Egypt
with a mighty hand, with an outstretched arm,
and with great awe,
and with signs and wonders."

The Lord took us out of Egypt
not by an angel and not by a seraph
and not by an agent.
Rather, it was the Holy One, blessed is He,
all by Himself.

As it is said
"That night I will pass through the land of Egypt,
and I will smite every firstborn in the land of Egypt,
whether man or beast,
and I will mete out justice to all the gods of Egypt.
I am the Lord."

וְאֶת עֲמָלֵנוּ – אֵלוּ הַבָּנִים.
כְּמָה שֶׁנֶּאֱמַר: כָּל הַבֵּן הַיִּלּוֹד הַיְאֹרָה תַּשְׁלִיכֻהוּ וְכָל הַבַּת תְּחַיּוּן.

וְאֶת לַחֲצֵנוּ – זוֹ הַדְּחַק
כְּמָה שֶׁנֶּאֱמַר: וְגַם רָאִיתִי אֶת הַלַּחַץ אֲשֶׁר מִצְרַיִם לֹחֲצִים אֹתָם.

וַיּוֹצִאֵנוּ יהוה מִמִּצְרַיִם
בְּיָד חֲזָקָה, וּבִזְרֹעַ נְטוּיָה, וּבְמֹרָא גָּדֹל וּבְאֹתוֹת וּבְמֹפְתִים.

וַיּוֹצִאֵנוּ יהוה מִמִּצְרַיִם
לֹא עַל יְדֵי מַלְאָךְ וְלֹא עַל יְדֵי שָׂרָף
וְלֹא עַל יְדֵי שָׁלִיחַ
אֶלָּא הַקָּדוֹשׁ בָּרוּךְ הוּא, בִּכְבוֹדוֹ וּבְעַצְמוֹ.

שֶׁנֶּאֱמַר: וְעָבַרְתִּי בְאֶרֶץ מִצְרַיִם בַּלַּיְלָה הַזֶּה
וְהִכֵּיתִי כָל בְּכוֹר בְּאֶרֶץ מִצְרַיִם
מֵאָדָם וְעַד בְּהֵמָה
וּבְכָל אֱלֹהֵי מִצְרַיִם אֶעֱשֶׂה שְׁפָטִים
אֲנִי יהוה.

"We cried out to the Lord, the God of our fathers,
and the Lord heard our voice,
and saw our affliction, our toil, and our oppression."

We cried out to the Lord, the God of our fathers
as it is said,
"It was during those many days
that the king of Egypt died,
and the children of Israel sighed from their servitude,
and they cried out,
and their cry rose up to God from their servitude."

And the Lord heard our voice – as it is said
"God heard their groaning,
and God remembered His covenant
with Abraham, with Isaac, and with Jacob."

And saw our affliction.
This refers to the disturbance of normal relationships,
as it is said,
"God saw the Children of Israel,
and God knew."

וַנִּצְעַק אֶל יהוה אֱלֹהֵי אֲבֹתֵינוּ
וַיִּשְׁמַע יהוה אֶת קֹלֵנוּ
וַיַּרְא אֶת עָנְיֵנוּ וְאֶת עֲמָלֵנוּ וְאֶת לַחֲצֵנוּ.

וַנִּצְעַק אֶל יהוה אֱלֹהֵי אֲבֹתֵינוּ
כְּמָה שֶׁנֶּאֱמַר:
וַיְהִי בַיָּמִים הָרַבִּים הָהֵם
וַיָּמָת מֶלֶךְ מִצְרַיִם
וַיֵּאָנְחוּ בְנֵי יִשְׂרָאֵל מִן הָעֲבֹדָה וַיִּזְעָקוּ
וַתַּעַל שַׁוְעָתָם אֶל הָאֱלֹהִים מִן הָעֲבֹדָה.

וַיִּשְׁמַע יהוה אֶת קֹלֵנוּ – כְּמָה שֶׁנֶּאֱמַר:
וַיִּשְׁמַע אֱלֹהִים אֶת נַאֲקָתָם
וַיִּזְכֹּר אֱלֹהִים אֶת בְּרִיתוֹ
אֶת אַבְרָהָם אֶת יִצְחָק וְאֶת יַעֲקֹב.

וַיַּרְא אֶת עָנְיֵנוּ.
זוֹ פְּרִישׁוּת דֶּרֶךְ אֶרֶץ, כְּמָה שֶׁנֶּאֱמַר:
וַיַּרְא אֱלֹהִים אֶת בְּנֵי יִשְׂרָאֵל
וַיֵּדַע אֱלֹהִים.

I passed by you,

and saw you wallowing in your own blood,

and I said to you, by your blood shall you live;

and I said to you, by your blood shall you live."

"The Egyptians were bad to us, and they afflicted us,

and they imposed hard work on us."

The Egyptians were bad to us – as it is said,

"Let us deal wisely with him,

lest he increase, and if there shall be a war,

he will also join with our enemies,

fight against us, and go up from the land."

And they afflicted us – as is is said,

"They set taskmasters over them

in order to afflict them with their burdens.

They built storage cities for Pharaoh:

Pithom and Raamses."

And they imposed hard work on us – as it is said,

"The Egyptians enslaved the children of Israel

with backbreaking work."

וָאֶעֱבֹר עָלַיִךְ וָאֶרְאֵךְ מִתְבּוֹסֶסֶת בְּדָמָיִךְ
וָאֹמַר לָךְ בְּדָמַיִךְ חֲיִי.
וָאֹמַר לָךְ בְּדָמַיִךְ חֲיִי.

וַיָּרֵעוּ אֹתָנוּ הַמִּצְרִים וַיְעַנּוּנוּ
וַיִּתְּנוּ עָלֵינוּ עֲבֹדָה קָשָׁה.

מגיד

וַיָּרֵעוּ אֹתָנוּ הַמִּצְרִים – כְּמוֹ שֶׁנֶּאֱמַר:
הָבָה נִתְחַכְּמָה לוֹ
פֶּן יִרְבֶּה, וְהָיָה כִּי תִקְרֶאנָה מִלְחָמָה
וְנוֹסַף גַּם הוּא עַל שֹׂנְאֵינוּ
וְנִלְחַם בָּנוּ, וְעָלָה מִן הָאָרֶץ.

וַיְעַנּוּנוּ – כְּמָה שֶׁנֶּאֱמַר:
וַיָּשִׂימוּ עָלָיו שָׂרֵי מִסִּים
לְמַעַן עַנֹּתוֹ בְּסִבְלֹתָם.
וַיִּבֶן עָרֵי מִסְכְּנוֹת לְפַרְעֹה
אֶת פִּתֹם וְאֶת רַעַמְסֵס.

וַיִּתְּנוּ עָלֵינוּ עֲבֹדָה קָשָׁה – כְּמוֹ שֶׁנֶּאֱמַר:
וַיַּעֲבִדוּ מִצְרַיִם אֶת בְּנֵי יִשְׂרָאֵל בְּפָרֶךְ.

He went down to Egypt –
compelled by the word of God.
And he dwelt there – this teaches
that our father Jacob did not go down
to settle in Egypt,
but rather only to live there temporarily, as it is said,
"They said to Pharaoh,
'we have come to live in the land

Maggid because there is no pasture for your servants' flocks,
because of the severe famine in the land of Canaan.
Now please let your servants dwell
in the Land of Goshen.'"
Few in number – as it is stated,
"As seventy souls
your ancestors came down to Egypt,
but now the Lord your God
has made you as numerous as the stars of the sky."
And there he became a nation
– this teaches that the Israelites excelled there.

Great, powerful – as it is said:
"And the Children of Israel were fruitful,
and increased abundantly,
and multiplied, and became very strong,
and the land was full of them."

And numerous – as it is said:
"I made you to increase like the growth of the field,
and you increased and grew, and became beautiful;
full breasts and hair grown long,
but you were naked and bare.

וַיֵּרֶד מִצְרַיְמָה – אָנוּס עַל פִּי הַדִּבּוּר.
וַיָּגָר שָׁם – מְלַמֵּד שֶׁלֹּא יָרַד יַעֲקֹב אָבִינוּ
לְהִשְׁתַּקֵּעַ בְּמִצְרַיִם
אֶלָּא לָגוּר שָׁם, שֶׁנֶּאֱמַר:
וַיֹּאמְרוּ אֶל פַּרְעֹה, לָגוּר בָּאָרֶץ בָּאנוּ
כִּי אֵין מִרְעֶה לַצֹּאן אֲשֶׁר לַעֲבָדֶיךָ
כִּי כָבֵד הָרָעָב בְּאֶרֶץ כְּנָעַן.
וְעַתָּה יֵשְׁבוּ נָא עֲבָדֶיךָ בְּאֶרֶץ גֹּשֶׁן.
בִּמְתֵי מְעָט – כְּמָה שֶׁנֶּאֱמַר:
בְּשִׁבְעִים נֶפֶשׁ יָרְדוּ אֲבוֹתֶיךָ מִצְרַיְמָה
וְעַתָּה שָׂמְךָ יהוה אֱלֹהֶיךָ כְּכוֹכְבֵי הַשָּׁמַיִם לָרֹב.
וַיְהִי שָׁם לְגוֹי – מְלַמֵּד שֶׁהָיוּ יִשְׂרָאֵל מְצֻיָּנִים שָׁם.

גָּדוֹל עָצוּם – כְּמוֹ שֶׁנֶּאֱמַר:
וּבְנֵי יִשְׂרָאֵל פָּרוּ וַיִּשְׁרְצוּ וַיִּרְבּוּ וַיַּעַצְמוּ בִּמְאֹד מְאֹד
וַתִּמָּלֵא הָאָרֶץ אֹתָם.

וָרָב – כְּמָה שֶׁנֶּאֱמַר:
רְבָבָה כְּצֶמַח הַשָּׂדֶה נְתַתִּיךְ
וַתִּרְבִּי וַתִּגְדְּלִי וַתָּבֹאִי בַּעֲדִי עֲדָיִים
שָׁדַיִם נָכֹנוּ וּשְׂעָרֵךְ צִמֵּחַ
וְאַתְּ עֵרֹם וְעֶרְיָה.

מגיד

as it is stated "He said to Abram,
'you should surely know that your seed
will be a stranger in a land not their own,
and they will serve them,
and they will afflict them for four hundred years.
Also, the nation that they shall serve I will judge,
and afterwards
they will depart with many possessions.'"

The leader raises his cup and says:

**And it is this promise that has stood for our ancestors
and for us.
Not only one oppressor has stood against us
to destroy us,
but rather in each generation,
they stand against us to destroy us,
but the Holy One, blessed be He,
saves us from their hand.**

He then then puts the cup down and continues:

**Go out and learn what Laban the Aramean
sought to do to our father Jacob.
Pharaoh only decreed death on the males,
but Laban sought to uproot everyone.
As it is stated,
"An Aramean sought to destroy my father;
he went down to Egypt,
and he dwelt there few in number,
and there he became a great nation,
powerful and numerous."**

שֶׁנֶּאֱמַר: וַיֹּאמֶר לְאַבְרָם, יָדֹעַ תֵּדַע
כִּי גֵר יִהְיֶה זַרְעֲךָ בְּאֶרֶץ לֹא לָהֶם
וַעֲבָדוּם וְעִנּוּ אֹתָם אַרְבַּע מֵאוֹת שָׁנָה.
וְגַם אֶת הַגּוֹי אֲשֶׁר יַעֲבֹדוּ דָּן אָנֹכִי
וְאַחֲרֵי כֵן יֵצְאוּ בִּרְכֻשׁ גָּדוֹל.

מגיד

מגביה את הכוס בידו, ואומר:

וְהִיא שֶׁעָמְדָה לַאֲבוֹתֵינוּ וְלָנוּ.
שֶׁלֹּא אֶחָד בִּלְבָד עָמַד עָלֵינוּ לְכַלּוֹתֵנוּ
אֶלָּא שֶׁבְּכָל דּוֹר וָדוֹר
עוֹמְדִים עָלֵינוּ לְכַלּוֹתֵנוּ
וְהַקָּדוֹשׁ בָּרוּךְ הוּא מַצִּילֵנוּ מִיָּדָם.

מניח הכוס וממשיך:

צֵא וּלְמַד מַה בִּקֵּשׁ לָבָן הָאֲרַמִּי
לַעֲשׂוֹת לְיַעֲקֹב אָבִינוּ.
שֶׁפַּרְעֹה לֹא גָזַר אֶלָּא עַל הַזְּכָרִים
וְלָבָן בִּקֵּשׁ לַעֲקוֹר אֶת הַכֹּל.
שֶׁנֶּאֱמַר: אֲרַמִּי אֹבֵד אָבִי
וַיֵּרֶד מִצְרַיְמָה, וַיָּגָר שָׁם בִּמְתֵי מְעָט
וַיְהִי שָׁם לְגוֹי גָּדוֹל עָצוּם וָרָב.

the only difference is time. If one produced his bread with alacrity, it is kosher for the holiday, but if he was lax, it becomes something else.

Further, as with all the other commandments of the seder, the physical demonstration is the main point. As we saw in the introduction, the main part of the Peasah is its physical consumption with the matza and bitter herbs, and the halacha declares that the meat and matza need to be prepared so that their true tastes are preserved. For example, cooked matza is disqualified because it no longer tastes as it should, and matza made with some supplemental rice or corn flour is disqualified if it no longer tastes like the true grain used in its preparation. Even the bitter herbs are referred to as such instead of their specific names, lettuce and chives, etc., because their taste is their purpose.

In the Laws of Leaven and Matza 6:12, Maimonides writes that the sages prohibited the consumption of matza on the day before Passover so that the consumption of matza on the night of the seder is noticeable (based on YT P'sahim 10:1). What prompted the sages to make such a prohibition, and why only with regard to matza, and not, for example, regarding the other foods that one is bidden to eat this night, like roasted lamb or goat, or bitter herbs, or perhaps even wine?

Concerning Yom Kippur, the Talmud teaches (B'rachoth 8b) that the main commandment of the tenth of the month of Tishrei, Yom Kippur, is to be observed "from the ninth of the month in the evening, from evening to evening," (Leviticus 23:32) thus connecting the holy day to the previous day, and because the unique commandment of the holy day is specifically to refrain from eating, we are obligated to do the opposite, i.e. to eat, on the preceding day, and one who does eat on Erev Yom Kippur is rewarded as if he fasted on Yom Kippur itself. By the same token, "In the first [month], on the fourteenth of the month in the evening, eat matzoth, until the twenty first day of the month, in the evening," (Exodus 12:18) means that we are to make sure not to eat matza on the fourteenth of Nisan. This explains how the sages knew to institute a prohibition against eating matza on Passover Eve, and to not make a similar prohibition against eating roasted goat's meat, wine, and bitter herbs on Passover eve: these latter foodstuffs are not mentioned in the critical verse.

Blessed is He who keeps His promise to Israel; blessed is He.
The Holy One, blessed be He,
pre-ordained the end of the servitude
in order to do as He said to our father Abraham
in the Covenant between the Parts,

Pharaoh responded by making a threat on Moses's life, but Moses had the last word:

"Moses said: 'You have spoken well; I will see your face again no more... Thus said the Lord: At about midnight will I go out into the midst of Egypt, and all the firstborn in the land of Egypt shall die, from the firstborn of Pharaoh who sits upon his throne until the firstborn of the maidservant who is behind the mill; and all the firstborn animals...'"

Moses finally described the most terrible wonder he had in store: the death of the firstborn. It is therefore surprising that, in advance of the final plague, God revealed more details to Moses:

"Speak to the entire congregation of Israel, saying: On the tenth day of this month they shall take to themselves every man a lamb, according to their fathers' houses, a lamb for a household... and you shall keep it until the fourteenth day of this month, and the whole assembly of the congregation of Israel shall slaughter it in the afternoon. For I will go through the land of Egypt that night, and I will smite all the firstborn in the land of Egypt, both man and beast, and against all the gods of Egypt I will execute judgments. I am the Lord."

The plague would also strike the gods of Egypt, that is, their idols, and the Israelites were also to be involved in the smiting. In contradiction to Moses's previous declarations, they were told specifically to take those Egyptian gods and slaughter them and ceremoniously display their blood.

Thus, the destruction of the leaven is an eternal memorial to this destruction of the Egyptian pantheon on the first Passover, and the consumption of the sacrifice is a memorial to Israel's victory over the Egyptian gods. It is the *s'or*, the sourdough in the dough that causes us to sin (B'rachoth 17), and when one neglects the performance of a commandment, he has "let it rise."

Leaven is forbidden from being part of the sacrifices brought on the altar, like anything that has been used in idolatrous service. Leaven has an advantage over any other class of food: it is the only everyday food that, from the outset of its production, can end up in one of two ways: leavened or unleavened, and

מגיד

בָּרוּךְ שׁוֹמֵר הַבְטָחָתוֹ לְיִשְׂרָאֵל, בָּרוּךְ הוּא.
שֶׁהַקָּדוֹשׁ בָּרוּךְ הוּא חִשַּׁב אֶת הַקֵּץ
לַעֲשׂוֹת כְּמוֹ שֶׁאָמַר לְאַבְרָהָם אָבִינוּ
בִּבְרִית בֵּין הַבְּתָרִים

and I led him through the entire land of Canaan.
I multiplied his seed, and I gave him Isaac,
and I gave Jacob and Esau to Isaac.
I gave Mount Seir to Esau, that he inherit it,
and Jacob and his children went down to Egypt."

Maggid

The Hebrews sought to journey three days from Egypt in order to sacrifice to their God, but Pharaoh would only allow them to go some distance from the Egyptian cities but within Egypt's borders. Pharaoh would also allow them the freedom to worship, a right which we take for granted in the modern era, but the freedom to leave was too much. Moses, arguing before Pharaoh's court, could not accept the offer:

'It is not right to do so, for shall we sacrifice the abomination of the Egyptians to the Lord our God? If we sacrifice the abomination of the Egyptians before their eyes, will they not stone us? We will go three days' journey into the wilderness, and sacrifice to the Lord our God as He shall command us.'

Moses asserted that he did not yet know what kind of sacrificial rite God would request. The Torah had yet to be given, and we will see that there were many commandments and laws which were so novel, some of the people had a hard time accepting them. Further, Moses did at least know that God would ask of them to slaughter of the sheep and goats, and it would be unthinkable for the Hebrews to use such for sacrifice while still in Egypt.

Then, after the plague of darkness, Pharaoh had one final offer:

'Go, serve the Lord; only let your flocks and your herds stay here; let your children also go with you.'

They could leave the country and worship as their God would please, but they would have to leave a deposit to ensure their return.

Moses said: 'You will also give us sacrifices and burnt-offerings, that we may sacrifice to the Lord our God. Our cattle also shall go with us; there shall not be a hoof left behind, for we must take from them to serve the Lord our God; and we will not know how we must serve the Lord until we get there.'

Indeed, the eventual mosaic law regarding sacrifices was much more restrictive than the codes that the patriarchs observed. For example, the mosaic law had higher standards of what is considered a disqualifying blemish, where altars and sanctuaries can be erected, who could officiate, and how altars could only be made from stones and dirt, but not one whole stone, from cut stones.

וָאוֹלֵךְ אוֹתוֹ בְּכָל אֶרֶץ כְּנָעַן וָאַרְבֶּה אֶת זַרְעוֹ וָאֶתֶּן לוֹ אֶת יִצְחָק וָאֶתֵּן לְיִצְחָק אֶת יַעֲקֹב וְאֶת עֵשָׂו. וָאֶתֵּן לְעֵשָׂו אֶת הַר שֵׂעִיר לָרֶשֶׁת אֹתוֹ וְיַעֲקֹב וּבָנָיו יָרְדוּ מִצְרָיִם.

In a number of essays printed in the Torah Sheleima to Parashat Bo, Rabbi Menachem Mendel Kasher wrote about the various prohibitions associated with leaven on Passover which parallel those of idolatry and its accouterments throughout the year. Both leaven and idolatrous objects may not remain in our possession, both must be destroyed, both are prohibited from being sources of benefit, and both are not subject to nullification in mixtures, and just like any idolatrous object that had ever been owned by a Jew can never be nullified and thereby used, the sages decreed that leaven that had been in a Jew's possession over Passover becomes forbidden forever. Indeed, there is much to be said about how leaven is, throughout the Talmudic and kabbalistic literature, a parable for the evil inclination in general and idolatry in particular.

Aren't the prohibition against leaven on Passover, and the requirement for its destruction, extreme? What has the bread done to deserve this? On the contrary, it is the staff of life all year round, and a critical component of every other sacramental meal, so why should it suffer such a horrible fate on Passover just because it symbolically represents idols? Why not treat some other class of foods as forbidden on Passover, say fruit, which is also forbidden as sacrifice, and create a host of symbolism around it?

The answer, I believe, lies in how the events of the Exodus unfolded.

Moses had been told about the forthcoming death of the firstborn when he first set out for Egypt:

The Lord said to Moses: 'When you go back to Egypt, see that you do all the wonders which I have put in your hand before Pharaoh; but I will harden his heart, and he will not let the people go. Then you shall say to Pharaoh: Thus says the Lord: Israel is My son, My firstborn. I have said to you: Let My son go, that he may serve Me, but you have refused to let him go. Behold, I will slay your son, your firstborn.'

Then after the plague of the multitude of wild animals, Pharaoh began to negotiate:

Pharaoh called for Moses and for Aaron, and said: 'Go, sacrifice to your God in the land.'

first month, on the fifteenth day of the first month; on the morrow of the Passover the children of Israel went out with a high hand in the sight of all the Egyptians," this being the essence of the Exodus from Moses's prophetic point of view, but in Joshua's point of view, the purpose of the Exodus was settling in the holy land, and the verses there have a number of Hebrew phrases used to describe the Exodus:

"The children of Israel encamped in Gilgal, and they kept the Passover on the fourteenth day of the month in the afternoon in the plains of Jericho. They ate of the *'avur*, the produce of the land on the morrow of the Passover, unleavened breads and parched grain, on that very day. The manna ceased on the morrow, after they had eaten of the produce of the land, and the children of Israel had no more manna, but they did eat of the yield of the land of Canaan that year."

According to Joshua, the very day of the Exodus, the day after the offering of the Pesah, was marked by the people's eating of the land's produce. This allows us to solve all of the previous difficulties. Matza is made from the grain that grows from the ground, while the maror itself is a form of vegetation, and the haroset used as a dip for the herbs is also made of vegetable products, but the sacrifice of Passover is an animal, and therefore not *'avur*, produce of the land. The verse in question should therefore be read: "with this produce, with which I once performed God's commandments, did the Lord do this for me when I left Egypt," and that is why the matza and maror, and not the meat of the sacrifice, need to be placed in front of him when he describes the Exodus.

It is worth noting that today those who immigrated to Israel from Western Europe and America appreciate the kabbalist-established Tu Bishvat seder in which they give God special thanks for the produce of the Land Israel, which is not present in the Diaspora.

Originally, our ancestors were idolaters,
but now, the Omnipresent
has brought us close to His service,
as it is stated, "Joshua said to all the people
so said the Lord, God of Israel:
Your ancestors used to dwell beyond the river,
Terah, the father of Abraham and the father of Nahor,
and they worshiped other gods.
I took your father, Abraham, from beyond the river,

The wording of the haggada is a little difficult. The verse just cited comes from a passage in the Torah that describes the seder with the Passover sacrifice (Exodus 13:8), so why doesn't the narrator say "when the **Pesah**, matza, and bitter herbs are actually placed in front of you?" Further, why does it say "placed in front of you?" After all, the commandment is to eat them, and therefore the haggada should read "when you **recline** to eat the Pesah, matza, and bitter herbs."

In his commentary to that verse, Ibn Ezra cites Ibn Janah who pointed out an apparent problem with the verse itself, which seems to say that God took the Israelites out of of Egypt for the sake of keeping the Passover commandments, that is, so that we keep the Passover commandments. Rabbi Marinus and others suggested that we should instead understand the verse as saying that we keep the Passover commandments because we were redeemed, but the Ibn Ezra rejected these suggestions because he could not fit them into the original wording of the verse.

In response, Nahmanides wrote that according to kabbala, it could be that God indeed brought about the Exodus so that we would perform the commandments, which serve to glorify His name in this world, and he brings other examples of this from scripture. However, this interpretation is still hard to see from the original wording of the verse.

The approaches of both Ibn Ezra and Nahmanides assume that the word in question, *ba'avur*, normally translated as "for the sake of," here implies some sort of causal relationship.

With regard to the purpose of the Exodus, the Torah says:

"It came to pass on that very day that the Lord brought the children of Israel out of the land of Egypt by their hosts," and "they journeyed from Rameses in the

מִתְּחִלָּה עוֹבְדֵי עֲבוֹדָה זָרָה הָיוּ אֲבוֹתֵינוּ

וְעַכְשָׁיו קֵרְבָנוּ הַמָּקוֹם לַעֲבֹדָתוֹ, שֶׁנֶּאֱמַר

וַיֹּאמֶר יְהוֹשֻׁעַ אֶל כָּל הָעָם

כֹּה אָמַר יהוה אֱלֹהֵי יִשְׂרָאֵל

בְּעֵבֶר הַנָּהָר יָשְׁבוּ אֲבוֹתֵיכֶם מֵעוֹלָם

תֶּרַח אֲבִי אַבְרָהָם וַאֲבִי נָחוֹר

וַיַּעַבְדוּ אֱלֹהִים אֲחֵרִים.

וָאֶקַּח אֶת אֲבִיכֶם, אֶת אַבְרָהָם, מֵעֵבֶר הַנָּהָר

and since he removed himself from the community,
he has denied a principle of the faith.
You should put him in his place and say to him,
"For the sake of this, did the Lord do this for me
when I left Egypt."
"For me," and not for him.
Had he been there, he would not have been redeemed.

Maggid What does the simple child say?
"What is this?"
You should say to him,
"With a mighty hand the Lord took us out of Egypt,
from the house of bondage."

And with the child who does not know how to ask,
you should prompt him, as it is stated,
"On that day, you shall tell your son, saying,
'for the sake of this, did the Lord do this for me
when I left Egypt.'"

Perhaps he should start
telling his children of the Exodus
already from the New Moon [of Nisan].
That is why the verse says "on that day."
If it is "on that day," perhaps it means
during the daytime [when the sacrifice is brought.]
That is why the verse says, "for the sake of this."
I only said "for the sake of this"
when matza and maror
are actually placed in front of you.

וּלְפִי שֶׁהוֹצִיא אֶת עַצְמוֹ מִן הַכְּלָל, כָּפַר בָּעִקָּר.
וְאַף אַתָּה הַקְהֵה אֶת שִׁנָּיו וֶאֱמָר לוֹ:
"בַּעֲבוּר זֶה עָשָׂה יהוה לִי בְּצֵאתִי מִמִּצְרָיִם."
לִי - וְלֹא לוֹ.
אִלּוּ הָיָה שָׁם, לֹא הָיָה נִגְאָל.

מגיד

תָּם, מַה הוּא אוֹמֵר?
"מַה זֹּאת?"
וְאָמַרְתָּ אֵלָיו
"בְּחֹזֶק יָד הוֹצִיאָנוּ יהוה מִמִּצְרַיִם מִבֵּית עֲבָדִים."

וְשֶׁאֵינוֹ יוֹדֵעַ לִשְׁאוֹל
אַתְּ פְּתַח לוֹ, שֶׁנֶּאֱמַר
"וְהִגַּדְתָּ לְבִנְךָ בַּיּוֹם הַהוּא לֵאמֹר
בַּעֲבוּר זֶה עָשָׂה יהוה לִי בְּצֵאתִי מִמִּצְרָיִם."

יָכוֹל מֵרֹאשׁ חֹדֶשׁ?
תַּלְמוּד לוֹמַר בַּיּוֹם הַהוּא.
אִי בַּיּוֹם הַהוּא, יָכוֹל מִבְּעוֹד יוֹם?
תַּלְמוּד לוֹמַר "בַּעֲבוּר זֶה."
"בַּעֲבוּר זֶה" לֹא אָמַרְתִּי
אֶלָּא בְּשָׁעָה שֶׁיֵּשׁ מַצָּה וּמָרוֹר מֻנָּחִים לְפָנֶיךָ.

until Ben Zoma explicated it, as it is said,
"So that you remember
the day of your leaving the land of Egypt
all the days of your life."
"The days of your life," refers to the daytime,
while "all the days of your life"
refers to the nighttime.
But the sages say, "the days of your life" is this world;
"all the days of your life" refers to the Messianic era.

Blessed is the Omnipresent, Blessed is He;
Blessed is the One Who gave the Torah
to His people Israel. Blessed is He.
The Torah spoke of four types of children:
one who is wise, one who is evil,
one who is simple,
and one who does not know how to ask.

What does the wise child say?
"What are these testimonies, statutes, and laws
that the Lord our God commanded you?"
You should say to him,
"as per the laws of the paschal offering;
We do not eat any kind of dessert
after the paschal offering."

What does the evil child say?
"What is this service of yours?"
"Yours," and not his,

עַד שֶׁדְּרָשָׁהּ בֶּן זוֹמָא, שֶׁנֶּאֱמַר
לְמַעַן תִּזְכֹּר אֶת יוֹם צֵאתְךָ מֵאֶרֶץ מִצְרַיִם
כֹּל יְמֵי חַיֶּיךָ. יְמֵי חַיֶּיךָ הַיָּמִים
כֹּל יְמֵי חַיֶּיךָ הַלֵּילוֹת.
וַחֲכָמִים אוֹמְרִים יְמֵי חַיֶּיךָ הָעוֹלָם הַזֶּה
כֹּל יְמֵי חַיֶּיךָ לְהָבִיא לִימוֹת הַמָּשִׁיחַ.

מגיד

בָּרוּךְ הַמָּקוֹם, בָּרוּךְ הוּא
בָּרוּךְ שֶׁנָּתַן תּוֹרָה לְעַמּוֹ יִשְׂרָאֵל, בָּרוּךְ הוּא.
כְּנֶגֶד אַרְבָּעָה בָנִים דִּבְּרָה תוֹרָה:
אֶחָד חָכָם, וְאֶחָד רָשָׁע
וְאֶחָד תָּם, וְאֶחָד שֶׁאֵינוֹ יוֹדֵעַ לִשְׁאוֹל.

חָכָם, מָה הוּא אוֹמֵר?
"מָה הָעֵדוֹת וְהַחֻקִּים וְהַמִּשְׁפָּטִים
אֲשֶׁר צִוָּה יהוה אֱלֹהֵינוּ אֶתְכֶם?"
וְאַף אַתָּה אֱמֹר לוֹ "כְּהִלְכוֹת הַפֶּסַח:
אֵין מַפְטִירִין אַחַר הַפֶּסַח אֲפִיקוֹמָן."

רָשָׁע, מָה הוּא אוֹמֵר?
"מָה הָעֲבוֹדָה הַזֹּאת לָכֶם?"
לָכֶם - וְלֹא לוֹ.

The leader answers:

Maggid

We were slaves to Pharaoh in the land of Egypt,
and the Lord, our God, took us out from there
with a strong hand and an outstretched arm.
Had the Holy One, blessed be He,
not taken our ancestors out of Egypt
then we, and our children,
and our children's children,
would be enslaved to Pharaoh in Egypt.
Even if we were all scholars, if we were all wise,
if we were all elders, if all of us knew the Torah,
it would be incumbent upon us
to tell the story of the exodus from Egypt.
The more one recounts
the story of the exodus from Egypt, the better.

Once, Rabbi Eliezer, Rabbi Yehoshua,
Rabbi Elazar ben Azaria,
Rabbi Akiva, and Rabbi Tarfon
were reclining in Bnei Brak,
and they were recounting the exodus from Egypt
that whole night,
until their students came and said to them,
"Our Masters, the time has come
for [reciting] the morning Shema."

Rabbi Elazar ben Azaria said,
Although I am like a seventy-year-old man,
I have not merited [to understand why] the exodus
from Egypt should be mentioned every night,

הקורא עונה:

עֲבָדִים הָיִינוּ לְפַרְעֹה בְּמִצְרָיִם
וַיּוֹצִיאֵנוּ יהוה אֱלֹהֵינוּ מִשָּׁם
בְּיָד חֲזָקָה וּבִזְרֹעַ נְטוּיָה.
וְאִלּוּ לֹא הוֹצִיא הַקָּדוֹשׁ בָּרוּךְ הוּא
אֶת אֲבוֹתֵינוּ מִמִּצְרַיִם
הֲרֵי אָנוּ וּבָנֵינוּ וּבְנֵי בָנֵינוּ
מְשֻׁעְבָּדִים הָיִינוּ לְפַרְעֹה בְּמִצְרָיִם.
וַאֲפִילוּ כֻּלָּנוּ חֲכָמִים כֻּלָּנוּ נְבוֹנִים
כֻּלָּנוּ זְקֵנִים כֻּלָּנוּ יוֹדְעִים אֶת הַתּוֹרָה
מִצְוָה עָלֵינוּ לְסַפֵּר בִּיצִיאַת מִצְרָיִם.
וְכָל הַמַּרְבֶּה לְסַפֵּר בִּיצִיאַת מִצְרַיִם הֲרֵי זֶה מְשֻׁבָּח.

מגיד

מַעֲשֶׂה בְּרַבִּי אֱלִיעֶזֶר וְרַבִּי יְהוֹשֻׁעַ
וְרַבִּי אֶלְעָזָר בֶּן עֲזַרְיָה וְרַבִּי עֲקִיבָא וְרַבִּי טַרְפוֹן
שֶׁהָיוּ מְסֻבִּין בִּבְנֵי בְרַק
וְהָיוּ מְסַפְּרִים בִּיצִיאַת מִצְרַיִם כָּל אוֹתוֹ הַלַּיְלָה
עַד שֶׁבָּאוּ תַלְמִידֵיהֶם וְאָמְרוּ לָהֶם
רַבּוֹתֵינוּ, הִגִּיעַ זְמַן קְרִיאַת שְׁמַע שֶׁל שַׁחֲרִית.

אָמַר רַבִּי אֶלְעָזָר בֶּן עֲזַרְיָה
הֲרֵי אֲנִי כְּבֶן שִׁבְעִים שָׁנָה
וְלֹא זָכִיתִי שֶׁתֵּאָמֵר יְצִיאַת מִצְרַיִם בַּלֵּילוֹת

is nothing unique about eating lamb or goat meat, and neither were prohibited on Passover Eve. The sages learned from the biblical description of the matza as *lehem 'oni*, poor bread, that it also alludes to *'aniya*, the act of answering, that is, the matza is supposed to stimulate discussion, indicating that the father should begin the discussion by introducing the matza, which is why we have made the editorial decision to leave at least the first sentence of the *Ha Lahma 'Anya* as it is. On the other hand, it can be argued that the *Ha Lahma 'Anya* was to be said upon presenting the matza that had been broken for the sake of producing the *afikoman*, which was eaten as a replacement for the Korban Pesah, and thus the entire section should now be omitted, and it is sufficient to bring the Pesah to the table and begin the discussion there.

Maggid

The child should then ask:

How is this night different from all [other] nights?
Every night we eat leavened and unleavened bread;
tonight, only unleavened bread.
Every night we eat assorted vegetables;
tonight, [only] bitter ones.
Every night we eat
roasted, stewed, or cooked meat;
tonight, only roasted.
Every night, we do not even dip [our food] once;
tonight, [we dip] twice.
Every night, we eat either sitting or reclining;
tonight, we all recline.

no Pesah, there is no specific prohibition to eat any other roasted meat at the seder, and that which existed in the Diaspora, that they did not eat any roasted meat the night of the seder, is a cautionary custom lest some suspect the participants of eating paschal meat. It is universally prohibited to eat a whole roasted kid, goat, or young lamb outside of Jerusalem the night of the seder, as it would look like the participants are eating sacrificial food.

The exilic text of the previous paragraph, known by its initial words, *Ha Lahma 'Anya*, continues with an invitation to those who need to join the seder, and a poetic prayer for the Redemption: "this year we are slaves, next year we shall be free; this year here, next year in Jerusalem." Obviously, the old text cannot be recited because we should not be inviting new participants who were not registered for the Pesah before the holiday began, no matter how needy they are. Moreover, even when the Pesah is present, the child's first question is regarding the commandments to eat matza and be rid of the leaven, because most of the preparations leading up to the holiday involved those commandments, and it has been an entire day that he was unable to eat both matza and leaven, and there

מגיד

וכאן הבן שואל:

מַה נִּשְׁתַּנָּה הַלַּיְלָה הַזֶּה מִכָּל הַלֵּילוֹת?

שֶׁבְּכָל הַלֵּילוֹת אָנוּ אוֹכְלִין חָמֵץ וּמַצָּה.

הַלַּיְלָה הַזֶּה כֻּלּוֹ מַצָּה.

שֶׁבְּכָל הַלֵּילוֹת אָנוּ אוֹכְלִין שְׁאָר יְרָקוֹת.

הַלַּיְלָה הַזֶּה כֻּלּוֹ מָרוֹר.

שֶׁבְּכָל הַלֵּילוֹת אָנוּ אוֹכְלִין

בָּשָׂר צָלִי שָׁלוּק וּמְבֻשָּׁל.

הַלַּיְלָה הַזֶּה כֻּלּוֹ צָלִי.

שֶׁבְּכָל הַלֵּילוֹת אֵין אָנוּ מַטְבִּילִין אֲפִילוּ פַּעַם אֶחָת.

הַלַּיְלָה הַזֶּה שְׁתֵּי פְעָמִים.

שֶׁבְּכָל הַלֵּילוֹת אָנוּ אוֹכְלִין בֵּין יוֹשְׁבִין וּבֵין מְסֻבִּין.

הַלַּיְלָה הַזֶּה כֻּלָּנוּ מְסֻבִּין.

The third question appears in the Mishna, and it is not asked when the Pesah is absent, because only the sacrificial meat has a required mode of cooking, whereas at a Pesah-less seder, the victuals may be prepared in any manner. When there is

**Any of the foods served on the table
with the Korban Pesah
need to be disposed of with it,
and may only be eaten until midnight,
like the Korban Pesah itself,
an enactment due to [the possibility of] mingling.**

See the introduction regarding the idea that the Jewish home is transformed into a sanctuary during the seder.

Karpas

Take some of the karpas and dip it in the haroset (or vinegar, or salt water according to various traditions), and recite the blessing:

**Blessed are You, O Lord, our God,
King of the universe,
Creator of the fruit of the ground.**

Eat the karpas.

Yahatz is no longer part of the seder because it is for the purpose of preparing the mazta to be eaten in lieu of the Korban Pesah.

Maggid

The seder plate is removed from before the leader (but not from the beyond the room) and pour the second cup. The leader points to the matzot and says:

**We left Egypt in a hurry.
This is the poor bread
that our ancestors ate in the land of Egypt.**

וְכָל הַתַּבְשִׁילִין הָעוֹלִים עִם הַפֶּסַח עַל הַשֻּׁלְחָן
מִתְבַּעֲרִין עִמּוֹ
וְאֵינָן נֶאֱכָלִים אֶלָּא עַד חֲצוֹת כַּפֶּסַח עַצְמוֹ
גְּזֵרָה, מִפְּנֵי הַתַּעֲרֹבֶת.

וראה בקונטרס המקדים עניין הבית היהודי כמקדש בשעת אכילת הפסח.

כַּרְפַּס

לוקח כזית מן הכרפס וטובלו בחרוסת, ומברך:

בָּרוּךְ אַתָּה יהוה, אֱלֹהֵינוּ מֶלֶךְ הָעוֹלָם
בּוֹרֵא פְּרִי הָאֲדָמָה.

ואוכלו. ולשיטת הבית יוסף אין לטבלו בחרוסת אלא בחומץ, ומנהג אשכנז שמטבילים במי מלח.

ופשוט שאין יַחַץ כי לא צריכים את המצה לצפון-אפיקומן,
כי היא באה במקום הפסח.

מַגִּיד

מסירים את המגש ובשר הקרבנות רק מלפני קורא ההגדה,
ומוזגין הכוס השני.
הקורא מצביע על המצות ואומר:

בְּבְהִילוּ יָצָאנוּ מִמִּצְרָיִם.
הָא לַחְמָא עַנְיָא
דִּי אֲכָלוּ אַבְהָתָנָא בְּאַרְעָא דְמִצְרָיִם.

This is the Passover offering that our ancestors ate in the land of Egypt, and it may only be eaten by those who registered for it beforehand.

Continue with a recitation of the laws of the Pesah as codified by Maimonides in order to warn the participants:

**Rabbi Moses Maimonides said:
Anyone who eats of the Korban Pesah
may only do so with one group
and none of it may be removed from that group.
One who moves an olive-sized amount of the sacrifice
between groups on the night of the fifteenth [of Nisan],
is punished with lashes.
As it is said, "do not remove any of the meat
from the house to the outside."
That is, he places it outside,
as "removal" is the standard in this case,
just like the [prohibition of removing items
into the public domain on] the Sabbath.
Therefore, the threshold for liability also includes
an act of removal and placement,
just like on the Sabbath.
There is no liability
for removing meat that had already been removed,
because once it has been removed initially,
it has already been disqualified.
Meat of the Korban Pesah that has left its group
whether through one's intentional or unwitting action,
becomes forbidden for consumption,
and is like meat of the most holy sacrifices
that left the [Temple] courtyard,
or the meat of less holy sacrifices
that left Jerusalem's walls,
which are both like non-kosher meat,
which carries the penalty of lashes for its consumption.**

הצגת הפסח

הָא דִיבַח חָיָס דִי אֲכָלוּ אַבְהָתָנָא בְּאַרְעָא דְמִצְרַיִם, וְלֵית הוּא מִתְאֲכִיל אֶלָּא לִמְנוּיוֹהִי.

ופירושו בעברית:

זֶה קָרְבַּן הַפֶּסַח שֶׁאָכְלוּ אֲבוֹתֵינוּ בְּאֶרֶץ מִצְרַיִם, וְאֵינֶנּוּ נֶאֱכָל אֶלָּא לִמְנוּיָיו.

קוראים מדברי הרמב״ם כדי להזהיר את המסובים:

אָמַר הָרַב מֹשֶׁה בֶּן מַיְמוֹן
כָּל הָאוֹכֵל מִן הַפֶּסַח
אֵינוֹ אוֹכֵל אֶלָּא בַּחֲבוּרָה אַחַת
וְאֵין מוֹצִיאִין מִמֶּנּוּ מִן הַחֲבוּרָה שֶׁיֵּאָכֵל בָּהּ.
וְהַמּוֹצִיא מִמֶּנּוּ כְּזַיִת בָּשָׂר מֵחֲבוּרָה לַחֲבוּרָה
בְּלֵילֵי חֲמִשָּׁה עָשָׂר, לוֹקֶה
שֶׁנֶּאֱמַר, לֹא תוֹצִיא מִן הַבַּיִת מִן הַבָּשָׂר חוּצָה.
וְהוּא שֶׁיַּנִּיחוֹ בַּחוּץ
שֶׁהוֹצָאָה כְּתוּבָה בּוֹ, כְּשַׁבָּת.
לְפִיכָךְ צָרִיךְ עֲקִירָה וְהַנָּחָה, כְּהוֹצָאַת שַׁבָּת.
וְאֵין מוֹצִיא אַחַר מוֹצִיא בַּפֶּסַח
שֶׁכֵּיוָן שֶׁהוֹצִיאוּ הָרִאשׁוֹן, נִפְסַל.
בְּשַׂר הַפֶּסַח שֶׁיָּצָא חוּץ לַחֲבוּרָתוֹ
בֵּין בְּזָדוֹן בֵּין בִּשְׁגָגָה, נֶאֱסַר בַּאֲכִילָה
וַהֲרֵי הוּא כִּבְשַׂר קָדְשֵׁי קָדָשִׁים שֶׁיָּצָא חוּץ לָעֲזָרָה
אוֹ בְשַׂר קָדָשִׁים קַלִּים שֶׁיָּצָא חוּץ לְחוֹמַת יְרוּשָׁלַיִם
שֶׁהַכֹּל טְרֵפָה, וְלוֹקִין עַל אֲכִילָתוֹ.

Urhatz

Wash your hands as you would normally before prayer and eating bread.

Because everything consumed with the sacrificial meat has to be eaten to sacrificial standards, those who intend to eat an olive-sized amount or more of karpas should ritually wash their hands and recite the usual blessing as though they were to eat bread, while those who intend to eat less should not recite the blessing upon washing their hands.

Hatzagat Hapesah

The seder plate, which should have the meat of the Korban Pesah and the other foods upon it, is brought to the table.

If one's hands are impure, he should immerse them in a mikveh and recite the appropriate blessing before bringing the Korban Pesah to the table. The meat of the Pesah should not be brought back out of the room, and if any meat is removed from the room, even by some force other than a person, it becomes disqualified and may not be eaten under any circumstances. Any disqualified meat should be saved for after Yom Tov, when it is to be burned along with any meat that may be left over after the meal.

> the prohibition begins when the meat is brought into the seder. Also, those who registered for a particular Korban Pesah may eventually split into groups for the seder, and because meat of the Korban must stay within the domain of its group, it makes sense that the requirement that it stay with its group only begins to exist when the group begins to exist. This indicates that the act that defines the group for the purposes of the seder, the Kiddush, is also the act that defines the place of the Pesah. Thus, the time of the Passover's consumption is limited to the time at which it is fit to be eaten, after it has been brought into the place where its group has gathered to eat it. According to the opinion of the Terumat Hadeshen mentioned in the introduction, viz., that the four cups can only be drunk when it is time to eat the Pesah, it may be argued that it is also the proper time to eat the Pesah once the Kiddush may be recited. Lastly, both the verse "it should be eaten in but one house," in the passive voice, and its negative counterpart, the verse, "do not take any of the meat out of the house," influence Maimonides's formulation: one should not remove the meat from its group's place, as every group has its own defined place with its own defined walls, just like the domains with regards to the laws against transferring between domains on the Sabbath. Therefore, we have proposed that the designated "place" of the Pesah for the purposes of this prohibition is limited to the room hosting the seder.

נוטלים לידים.

מכיוון שאוכלים בלילה זה קרבן פסח, אפילו אכילת החולין צריכה להיות על טהרת הקודש והנטילה חובה, אז אלה שמתכוונים לאכול כזית בכרפס או יותר יטלו ידיהם עם ברכת "על נטילת ידים," ואלה שלא יאכלו כזית יטלו בלי ברכה.

מביאים את הקערה שעליה בשר הפסח ושאר המאכלים לשולחן.

אם ידיו טמאות, יש לטבלן במקווה ולברך על טבילת ידים כדין קדשים לפני שמביא את הפסח אצל המסובים. אין להוציא מבשר הפסח מן החדר, ואם הוציא, נפסל הבשר ואסור לאוכלו. וכן אם יצא הבשר מאליו מן המקום, גם נפסל, וכגון שגררו עכבר, יש להשאירו עם שאר הבשר שיִוָּתֵר עד הבוקר, ולשרפם אחרי יום טוב.

From Yerushalmi P'sahim 7:13, it seems that there is no prohibition against taking meat of the Pesah out of its room before the time has come for the meat to be eaten, presumably after Maggid. However, from the text of the haggada itself we see that the prescribed time for the commandment to tell the Passover story is from when the matza and maror are on the table, and it is reasonable to assume that the time for consuming the Pesah coincides with the time for telling the story. Further, according to strict Torah law, one may eat the Pesah and tell the story in whatever order he wishes, and it is merely a rabbinic enactment that one drink two cups of wine and recite the body of the haggada before eating the Pesah, matza, and maror. Alternatively, the entire seder, beginning with the Kiddush, is considered the time for consumption of the Pesah, to the exclusion of any earlier time, during the preparation for the seder. It is clear that at some point it is permissible to move the meat from place to place: the Korban Pesah is slaughtered within the Temple courtyard, a closed domain, and then from there brought out into the the outer courts and the rest of the Temple Mount, which are also defined domains, and brought to wherever it is to be roasted before finally being brought to the seder table within yet another defined domain. Maimonides writes that the Pesah is brought in front of the participants from its preparation place only after they have sat and drunk the first cup, implying that once again,

Kaddesh **in memory of the Exodus from Egypt.
For You chose us,
and You sanctified us among all the nations,
[on Shabbat: and the Sabbath]
and Your holy appointed times,
[on Shabbat: in love and favor,]
in happiness and rejoicing, You did grant us.
Blessed are You, O Lord,
Sanctifier of [on Shabbat: the Sabbath,]
Israel, and the seasons.**

On Saturday night, recite the blessings on a candle and upon the end of the Sabbath, respectively:

Blessed are You, O Lord, our God, King of the universe,
Creator of the illuminations of fire.

Blessed are You, O Lord, our God, King of the universe,
Who distinguishes between the sacred and the secular,
between light and darkness, between Israel and the nations,
between the seventh day and the six days of creation.
You have distinguished between the holiness
of the Sabbath and the holiness of the Festival,
and You have sanctified the seventh day
from among the six days of creation.
You have distinguished and sanctified
Your people Israel with Your holiness.
Blessed are You, O Lord,
Who distinguishes between holiness and holiness.

On all nights, conclude Kiddush with this blessing:

**Blessed are You, O Lord, our God, King of the universe,
who has given us life, and sustained us, and brought
us to this season.**

Drink the first cup in a reclining position.
(Some hold that reclining is no longer necessary.)

קַדֵּשׁ

זֵכֶר לִיצִיאַת מִצְרָיִם.
כִּי בָנוּ בָחַרְתָּ, וְאוֹתָנוּ קִדַּשְׁתָּ מִכָּל הָעַמִּים
(לשבת: וְשַׁבָּת) וּמוֹעֲדֵי קָדְשֶׁךָ
(לשבת: בְּאַהֲבָה וּבְרָצוֹן)
בְּשִׂמְחָה וּבְשָׂשׂוֹן הִנְחַלְתָּנוּ.
בָּרוּךְ אַתָּה יהוה
מְקַדֵּשׁ (לשבת: הַשַּׁבָּת וְ)יִשְׂרָאֵל וְהַזְּמַנִּים.

במוצאי שבת מוסיפים ברכה על הנר והבדלה:

בָּרוּךְ אַתָּה יהוה, אֱלֹהֵינוּ מֶלֶךְ הָעוֹלָם
בּוֹרֵא מְאוֹרֵי הָאֵשׁ.

בָּרוּךְ אַתָּה יהוה, אֱלֹהֵינוּ מֶלֶךְ הָעוֹלָם
הַמַּבְדִּיל בֵּין קֹדֶשׁ לְחֹל, בֵּין אוֹר לְחֹשֶׁךְ
בֵּין יִשְׂרָאֵל לָעַמִּים
בֵּין יוֹם הַשְּׁבִיעִי לְשֵׁשֶׁת יְמֵי הַמַּעֲשֶׂה.
בֵּין קְדֻשַּׁת שַׁבָּת לִקְדֻשַּׁת יוֹם טוֹב הִבְדַּלְתָּ
וְאֶת יוֹם הַשְּׁבִיעִי מִשֵּׁשֶׁת יְמֵי הַמַּעֲשֶׂה קִדַּשְׁתָּ.
הִבְדַּלְתָּ וְקִדַּשְׁתָּ אֶת עַמְּךָ יִשְׂרָאֵל בִּקְדֻשָּׁתֶךָ.
בָּרוּךְ אַתָּה יהוה, הַמַּבְדִּיל בֵּין קֹדֶשׁ לְקֹדֶשׁ.

בכל הימים מסיימים עם ברכת הזמן:

בָּרוּךְ אַתָּה יהוה, אֱלֹהֵינוּ מֶלֶךְ הָעוֹלָם
שֶׁהֶחֱיָנוּ, וְקִיְּמָנוּ, וְהִגִּיעָנוּ לַזְּמַן הַזֶּה.

שותה בהסיבת שמאל ואינו מברך ברכה אחרונה.

אם יושבים ליד שלחן עם כסאות של ימינו, יש אומרים שלא צריכים להסב.

Kaddesh

Kaddesh

Pour the first cup of wine, and recite the Kiddush upon it.

On the night of Shabbat, begin Kiddush with this paragraph:

There was evening and there was morning,
the sixth day.
The heaven and the earth and all their host were finished.
On the seventh day God finished His work
which He had done,
and He rested on the seventh day from all His work
which He had done.
God blessed the seventh day and sanctified it
for on it He rested from all of His work
which God created by doing.

On other nights, begin Kiddush with this paragraph:

**Blessed are You, O Lord, our God,
King of the universe,
Creator of the fruit of the vine.**

**Blessed are You, O Lord, our God,
King of the universe,
who has chosen us from among all nations,
and has raised us above all languages,
and has sanctified us with His commandments.
You, O Lord, our God, have lovingly given us,
[on Shabbat: Sabbaths for rest],
appointed times for happiness,
festivals and seasons for rejoicing,
[on Shabbat: this Sabbath day, and]
this day of the Festival of Matzot,
our season of freedom,
a holy convocation** [on Shabbat: **of love**]

קַדֵּשׁ

מוזגין הכוס הראשון ומקדשים.

בשבת מתחילין כאן:

וַיְהִי עֶרֶב וַיְהִי בֹקֶר יוֹם הַשִּׁשִּׁי.
וַיְכֻלּוּ הַשָּׁמַיִם וְהָאָרֶץ וְכָל צְבָאָם.
וַיְכַל אֱלֹהִים בַּיּוֹם הַשְּׁבִיעִי מְלַאכְתּוֹ אֲשֶׁר עָשָׂה
וַיִּשְׁבֹּת בַּיּוֹם הַשְּׁבִיעִי מִכָּל מְלַאכְתּוֹ אֲשֶׁר עָשָׂה.
וַיְבָרֶךְ אֱלֹהִים אֶת יוֹם הַשְּׁבִיעִי, וַיְקַדֵּשׁ אוֹתוֹ
כִּי בוֹ שָׁבַת מִכָּל מְלַאכְתּוֹ אֲשֶׁר בָּרָא אֱלֹהִים לַעֲשׂוֹת.

בחול מתחילין כאן:

סַבְרִי מָרָנָן וְרַבָּנָן וְרַבּוֹתַי.
בָּרוּךְ אַתָּה יהוה, אֱלֹהֵינוּ מֶלֶךְ הָעוֹלָם,
בּוֹרֵא פְּרִי הַגָּפֶן.

בָּרוּךְ אַתָּה יהוה, אֱלֹהֵינוּ מֶלֶךְ הָעוֹלָם
אֲשֶׁר בָּחַר בָּנוּ מִכָּל עָם, וְרוֹמְמָנוּ מִכָּל לָשׁוֹן
וְקִדְּשָׁנוּ בְּמִצְוֹתָיו.
וַתִּתֶּן לָנוּ יהוה אֱלֹהֵינוּ בְּאַהֲבָה
(לשבת: שַׁבָּתוֹת לִמְנוּחָה וּ)
מוֹעֲדִים לְשִׂמְחָה, חַגִּים וּזְמַנִּים לְשָׂשׂוֹן.
(לשבת: אֶת יוֹם הַשַּׁבָּת הַזֶּה וְ)
אֶת יוֹם חַג הַמַּצּוֹת הַזֶּה, זְמַן חֵרוּתֵנוּ,
(לשבת: בְּאַהֲבָה) מִקְרָא קֹדֶשׁ

The Passover Seder

The Seder Plate:

The Seder Plate is arranged with portions of bitter herbs, karpas, haroset, the meat of the Korban Pesah, and, if present, the meat of the Korban Hagiga. Two whole matzot accompany the Seder Plate.

The sages ordained that every participant also drink four cups of wine as prescribed throughout the seder, and therefore sufficient wine should also be ready. According to the Shulhan Aruch, grape juice counts as wine.

Those who registered with a particular Korban Pesah may separate themselves into smaller groups for the seder, but those groups should not mingle with each other, or, for that matter, with any groups made of those who registered with other Pesahim, until after the drinking of the third cup of wine.

The Seder Without the Korban Pesah	The Seder With the Korban Pesah
Kaddesh	**Kaddesh**
Urhatz	**Urhatz**
Karpas ← *Hatzagat Hapesah*	**(Hatzagat Hapesah)**
~~Yahatz~~	**Karpas**
Maggid	**Maggid**
Rohtza	**Rohtza**
Motzi Matza	**Motzi Matza**
Maror ← *Hagiga*	**Maror**
~~Korech~~ ← *Pesah*	**(Hagiga)**
Shulhan Oreich	**(Pesah)**
~~Tzafun~~	**Shulhan Oreich**
Bareich	**Bareich**
Hallel ← *Birkat Hashir*	**Hallel**
Nirtza	**(Birkat Hashir)**
	Nirtza

how to by God (Exodus 10:26), or because they at least knew that they were to sacrifice sheep, but would not dare to do so in Egypt because of the Egyptians' reaction (*ibid.*, 8:22), after the plague of darkness, Moses commanded the people to indeed offer sacrifices in Egypt, which certainly seemed puzzling to many and contradicted his previous statements, which would have impugned his reputation as a true prophet, but the people still trusted him. Ultimately, it was in the merit of the observance of the Passover offering that they left Egypt.

The third surprise/novelty was that Moses ordered the people to build a portable sanctuary even before they arrived in the land of Israel, and this was because of the people's critical need for a physical medium of worship. The permanent Temple was already on their minds when they sang at the sea, "The Sanctuary, O Lord, that Your hands established," and the commandment to bring the choicest first fruits "to the Temple of the Lord your God" preceded the commandment to contribute toward the construction of the Tabernacle. It seems, as per the Midrash, that had the people not sinned with the Calf, they would have entered the land immediately after Moses came down from the mount, and the conquest and the building of the Temple would have soon followed, but it was not to be. Thus, each of these critical events, receiving the Torah at Sinai, offering sacrifices in Egypt, and the erection of the Tabernacle before arriving in the promised land, preceded the stages of the Redemption, and perhaps foreshadow our own destiny and the unfolding of our Redemption.

> *caused by the desire for the priesthood. Therefore, it was commanded that the Temple should not be built before the election of a king who would order its construction, and thus remove the root of potential conflict, as we have explained in the Book of Judges.*

(The reference is to his own book, not the biblical book, Judges.)

In *Or Hameir* by Rabbi Ze'ev Wolf of Zhitomir, a student of the Maggid of Mezrich, we find the following in his comments to Parashat Teruma:

> *This has persisted in every generation, that we, the children of Israel, are destined to build a new storey of the Sanctuary of the divine presence... The verse says, "they shall build a sanctuary for Me, and I will dwell among them." It does not say "I will dwell in it," but rather, "I will dwell among them," which teaches that the Holy One, blessed is He, dwells within every Jew... and this is what the Zohar means when it says, "the image of Creation, the image of the Tabernacle, and the image of a human being are one."*

XIII. The Historical Novelty of Moses

The book of Exodus describes three surprising narratives concerning the Torah, the sacrificial service, and the building of the Temple. Regarding the Torah, our forefathers were told in advance about the servitude and the Redemption, and Joseph's brothers knew likewise after he told them, "I am dying, but God will definitely recall you and bring you up from this land to the land which He swore to Abraham, Isaac, and Jacob." Yet, when he first heard God's voice from the burning bush, Moses received instructions that did not fit the plan. Instead of bringing the Israelites directly to Canaan, he was to bring them to Sinai to worship God and receive the commandments of the Torah. The people should have been taken aback by this development, as they were expecting to return to the promised land, but they still believed in Moses's agency.

The second surprise was that although Moses explicitly told the people and Pharaoh that they would not offer sacrifices in Egypt, either because they did not know how to do so and had yet to be told ones that bring about the sanctification of the individual as a Jew, and therefore we find all of these factors regarding Abraham and Isaac, whose acts of circumcision and sacrifice were mentioned above, and whose immersions in the purifying *miqweh* waters are also alluded to in the verses. With regards to Abraham, he invited his guests to "wash your feet and recline under the tree," on which the Zohar comments that Abraham regularly encouraged his guests, that is, those whom he wished to convert to monotheism, to wash themselves in the waters found near his tree, while with regard to Isaac we read that "Isaac's servants dug in the valley, and found there a well of living waters... he built an altar there, and called upon the name of the Lord, and pitched his tent there; and there Isaac's servants dug a well," which plainly refers to a source of drinking water, but midrashically/metaphorically refers to a place of Torah study, as above, or slightly more literally, to a place of ritual immersion and purification.

XII. Closeness to God and Anticipation of Redemption

Every Jewish soul yearns to come closer to God's service, and every Jew really wants to be like one of the kohanim, standing in the Divine Presence, and this was alluded to Moses's prayer, "if only all of the Lord's people were prophets, that the Lord would place His spirit upon them." This idea explains why some commentators seek to portray the spies as unwitting sinners, as they sought to prolong their study of the Torah without the interruptions and worldly hassles engendered by building a Jewish state. Others argue that Korah and his party sought to take the places of Moses and Aaron, to hold positions of Torah-leadership and priesthood, and when the people made the golden calves, both at Sinai and in Jeroboam's days, it was for the sake of Heaven. How much more so can it be said regarding the intentions of those who did not actually sin, who only desire the opportunity to enter a place of holiness! Maimonides explains why it was necessary to appoint a king in Israel before the construction of the Temple (Guide, 3:45):

> *Thirdly, and most importantly, every one of the twelve tribes would have wanted to have the Temple within its territory and under its control; this would lead to divisions and discord, such as were*

Tov when they are performed at their prescribed times.

Both circumcision and sacrifice are performed only during the daytime, and ideally right at the beginning of the day, and both should be done as soon as possible.

Circumcisions may be performed by any adult Jews, which technically includes women and "Canaanite" slaves, and similarly, the slaughter of all sacrifices may be performed by all.

Thus, circumcision is the only commandment that not only has blessings to be recited before the performance of the act, but also has a blessing to be recited upon a cup of wine afterward. Similarly, the sacrifices have a pre-performance blessing recited by the attending priests, and are followed by the singing of psalms upon the offering of the accompanying libations.

The bringing of the annual paschal sacrifice and the performance of the rite of circumcision are the only positive commandments that carry the penalty of *kareth*, excision from the rest of the nation, for one who fails to perform them.

We thus see that the sacrifices are the communal obligation to uphold the covenant, although each individual has a share in contributing toward the purchase of the sacrifices, while circumcision is the obligation incumbent on each and every individual, although the authorities can and should intervene, for example when a man refuses to have his children circumcised.

We also find that (Laws of Forbidden Relations 13):

> *Israel entered the covenant [with God] with three acts: circumcision, immersion, and offering a sacrifice. Circumcision took place in Egypt... Immersion was performed in the desert before the Giving of the Torah... Sacrifices [were also offered then], as it states: "And he sent out the youth of the children of Israel and they brought burnt offerings..." For [all] future generations, when a gentile desires to enter into the covenant, to take shelter under the wings of the Divine presence and accept the yoke of the Torah, he must undergo circumcision, immersion, and the offering of a sacrifice.*

That is, these two commandments, circumcision and sacrifice, are the

(12:43) and upon the beginning of Joshua's conquest (Joshua 5:1-10), and we find the words of the Midrash to Ezekiel 16:6 that connect these two commandments:

> *Rabbi Matthew ben Harash said that when the time came for the Exodus from Egypt, the Lord found the Israelites bereft of commandments to perform in order to merit redemption, and He therefore gave them the commandments of the blood of sacrifice and the blood of circumcision.*

Rabbi Aharon Ziegler reports that according to Rabbi J.B. Solovietchik, the Passover offering serves the identical function of circumcision throughout our history: it constitutes the mark of our collective Jewish identity.

Indeed, the halacha seems to equate circumcision with sacrifice, as all the laws of circumcision that have to do with the act of circumcision have their parallel in the laws of sacrifices:

With regard to sacrifices, the main act is the ritual of the blood, which has to be received by the priest and thrown on the altar, while with regard to circumcision, the drawing of the blood is the main act, and therefore, in cases where there is no foreskin, for example a child born without one or a convert who had previously been circumcised, blood must at least be drawn.

Only animals at least eight days old may be brought as sacrifices, and only children at least eight days old are eligible for circumcision.

Only animals that are *temimim*, unblemished, are to be made into sacrifices, and Abraham, when he was first given the commandment, was bidden by God to "walk before Me and be *tamim*," and as Rashi explains according to our sages, one who has a foreskin is considered to be blemished.

One who brings a sacrifice to the Temple celebrates the day as a personal Yom Tov, and one who circumcises his son also enjoys a personal Yom Tov, meaning that on that day he is exempted from a public fast and its attendant prohibitions.

The acts of circumcision and sacrifice override the Sabbath and Yom

of the relevant verses, the midrashic material, and, most importantly, the halacha, which, like in previous instances, draws an equivalence between sacrifice and circumcision.

The connections begin in Abraham's story: At first he was instructed just to go to the land God would show him (Genesis 12:1), and when he got there, God promised the land to his descendants (12:7). Later, God also promised the land to Abraham himself (13:15). Still later, God initiated a covenant with Abraham (15:18), to give the land of Canaan to him and his descendants, a covenant meaning that the gift would be eternal, and that it would be on condition that the people keep their side of the deal. As alluded to by the prophetic account of the Covenant Between the Parts, Abraham was taught that the Jewish people would merit the land through their offering of the Temple sacrifices. Then, some years later, God added another condition: that His people should circumcise themselves (17:10). Abraham dutifully did so, and shortly thereafter he was awarded by having the opportunity to once again offer sacrifice, but this time in the presence of three angelic visitors. Ultimately, the two commandments that Abraham performed on God's command, as tests of his faith, were to circumcise his son and to bring him as a sacrifice.

Therefore, because it is in the merit of both the sacrifices and circumcision that the Jewish people earn the right to possess the land of Israel, the texts of the prayers corresponding to the *musafim*, the additional communal offerings of the holidays, invoke the ingathering of the exiles, and the post-circumcision blessing does likewise:

> *Therefore, in this merit the living God, our portion, our redeemer, commanded to save our dear remnant from destruction for the sake of the sign of the covenant He sealed in our flesh.*

Saving the Jewish people is a liturgical expression for the ingathering of the exiles, as in I Chronicles 16:35:

> *And say: 'Save us, O God of our salvation, And gather us together and deliver us from the nations, that we may thank Your holy name, That we may triumph in Your praise.'*

Later, we see that the commandment of circumcision is directly connected to the fundamental paschal sacrifice, both before the Exodus

that the integrity of the Israelite houses they would occupy in Egypt would be maintained, such that they would remain holy enough to also serve as sanctuaries, and that one day God's Sanctuary would again be among them, as we wrote above. The proof for this can be found in the first passage that describes the daily offering in the Tabernacle of the wilderness (Exodus 29:)

> *It shall be a continual burnt-offering throughout your generations at the entrance of the Tent of Meeting before the Lord, where I will meet with you, to speak to you there. There I will meet with the children of Israel, and it shall be sanctified by My glory… I will dwell among the children of Israel, and I will be their God. They shall know that I am the Lord their God, who took them out of the land of Egypt so that I may dwell among them.*

XI. Circumcision and the Sacrificial Rite

Among the pre-circumcision rites found in the traditional Edot Hamizrah prayer book, you will find a recitation from the Zohar that equates the father's voluntarily bringing his son to the circumcision with an act of animal sacrifice. Thereafter, you will find a prayer for the father to recite, which asks that God accept the father's act as a "fragrant aroma," the biblical term used to describe a sacrifice that is accepted with favor, and a prayer for the sandak to recite, that he serve as a proper altar. In the Shulhan Aruch (Yoreh De'ah 264) it is written that if the father is not the mohel, he should stand over the mohel and observe the circumcision, because as the Vilna Gaon cites from the Tur, "how can it be someone's sacrifice is offered without his attending it?" a rhetorical question borrowed from the Mishna (Ta'anith 4:2) that describes the *ma'amad*, the regular rotational delegation of Israelites who would represent the people at the offering of the communal sacrifices, which was conducted by the priests on their behalf.

The Vilna Gaon also points to a Midrash in Vayikra Rabba (Emor 27) that draws a halachic similarity between the animal intended for sacrifice and the child to be circumcised. Like many other kabbalistic ideas and concepts we have seen before, this idea is implied by a careful reading of Abraham's traditions. This foreshadowed the Sanhedrin sitting in the Chamber of Hewn Stone adjacent to the Temple's courtyard, where the permanent altar sat.

X. The Restoration of the Sacrificial Service: Nahmanides's Main Theme in Exodus

In his commentary to Genesis 46:1, Nahmanides writes:

> *It was thus in the merit of the sacrifices that the God of his father Isaac appeared to him in "the visions of the night" through the (non-exacting) attribute of justice. It is this which Scripture says concerning "in the visions of the night," similar to that which He said [to Jacob earlier], "I am the God, the God of your father," for He is the God of Bethel Who said to him in Haran, "I am the God [who abides in] Bethel, where you anointed a pillar." He is the God of your father. This is the [divine] Name and it [represents] this [divine] attribute. He assured him that he would not fear [while] in Egypt, because he will be found worthy in the Divine judgment, and will be redeemed after the oppression. This is also the meaning of [God's] promise, "And I will also bring you up again." Now [Maimonides] has written in the twenty-seventh chapter of the first part of the Guide to the Perplexed that Onqelos's translation of the verse [I will go down with you, and I will also bring you up again] is rendered literally: "I will go down with you...and I will also bring you up again." Maimonides was surprised by Onqelos's [use of a literal anthropomorphism]... [Onqelos] wanted to allude to that which our sages said, "When they were exiled to Egypt, the Divine Presence went with them, as it is said, I will go down with you to Egypt. When they were exiled to Elam, the Divine Presence went down with them, as it is said, And I will set My throne in Elam..."*

Explanation: Jacob was afraid of going down to Egypt lest the Divine Presence not accompany him. That is, the main effects of having a central place of worship and divine revelation, of sacrifice and prophecy, can only be experienced in the Divine Presence. Jacob's tent in the land of Canaan was the sanctuary at that time, and God promised him was the designated place of the altar, sacrifice, pilgrimage, and divine revelation. When Abraham first received the revelation of the angels, he was sitting *pethah ha'ohel*, "[at] the entrance of the tent," once again, the Hebrew is missing the preposition, which alludes to the placement of Abraham's altar somewhere outside the tent, and when the angels delivered the news of Isaac's conception, it says "*w'sara shoma'ath pethah ha'ohel*, Sarah was listening [at] the entrance of the tent," i.e., she now occupied the place beside the altar that Abraham had occupied, indicating her involvement in the meditation and sacrifice, and resultant revelation.

With all of this in mind, we find that Parashat Wayeira is partially chiastic in that its conclusion is reminiscent of its opening. First we read about Abraham bringing a special form of sacrifice before God and then receiving word of Isaac's birth, and later we read about Abraham bringing a special sacrifice, the Binding of Isaac, and then receiving word of Rebecca's birth. And, in both accounts, a "lad" is mentioned as assisting Abraham, and in both instances, the sages identified that lad as Ishmael, who was made to observe and learn from both episodes.

Isaac continued Abraham's practices, "calling in the name of the Lord," so that all would know that the world has a Creator, and our sages saw allusions to Abraham's teachings in the incident of the dispute over the wells after Abraham's death (Genesis 26): "Now all the wells which his father's servants had dug in the days of his father Abraham, the Philistines had stopped them, and filled them with dirt," that is, the Philistines began to deny Abraham's teachings, and actively repudiated them, as though saying, "what are we to do with this Hebrew, Abraham, who uses kindness and charity to trick innocent people into serving his One God," but Isaac redug those wells, restoring Abraham's teachings, and the wells' water represents none other than "the well of living water," the Torah that was compared to water. There, at the edge of the promised land, God appeared to and blessed Isaac, and "he built an altar there, and called upon the name of the Lord, and pitched his tent there; and there Isaac's servants dug a well." Isaac also built an altar, and that is where he prayed, and that is where he had his tent, his sanctuary. His servants, who were essentially his loyal students, drew water from his well that was there, meaning the house of study, where they would learn

Your ministers," the fire being the angel that raises the sacrifice.

This idea, that Abraham experienced a detailed divine revelation while performing a form of sacrifice, is subtly described in Onqelos's translation. It says (18:8), "and he stood *['omed]* over them under the tree while they ate," which in Aramaic is rendered, "and he ministered [*m'shammeish*]," the same verb used in the subsequent books of the Pentateuch as the translation for the main activities of the priests, *la'avod* and *l'shareth*, and Onqelos does not use his usual, literal translation for *'omed*. Further, it says that when the "men" had finished their mission to Abraham (18:22), "the men turned from there, and went toward Sodom, but Abraham was still standing [*'odennu 'omed*] before the Lord," which is rendered, "but Abraham was still ministering in prayer [*m'shammeish bitzlo*] before the Lord." That is, when the sacrifice was being consumed by the fire, Abraham stood under the tree in prayer, and continued in that state when God informed him of Sodom's imminent destruction symbolized by the approach of the angels to the city, because the essential act of the sacrificial rite is the *kawwana*, the intention and concentration of the spirit brought about through prayer. Prayer and sacrifice go hand in hand, and it is only to our disadvantage that the divine service is missing. This point is reinforced after the upheaval of Sodom, when we read (19:27), "Abraham got up early in the morning" to look out upon Sodom, "to the place where he had stood [*asher 'amad sham*] before the Lord," and once again the translation is "where he had ministered in prayer."

This linguistic concept is most explicit in a verse (Deuteronomy 18:7), that, according to tradition (Rashi to *ibid*., 6), is referring to the subset of Levites known as Kohanim: "Then he shall serve, *w'shereth*, in the name of the Lord his God, as all his brethren the Levites do, who stand, *ha'om'dim*, there [in the Temple] before the Lord." Both of those critical Hebrew verbs describing the sacrificial service, serving and standing, are translated into Aramaic as *shimmush*, ministering. All of this being considered, we can postulate that the sages decreed that the main obligatory prayer, the *'amida*, be offered while standing because of its essential connection to the sacrifices.

Abraham and Sarah in essence turned their tent into **the** Sanctuary. It

IX. The Practice of Abraham and Sarah in the Sanctuary that Was Their Home

Zohar, Wayeira:

> *What is the meaning of [Genesis 18:4-8]: "Let now a little water be fetched, and wash your feet... And I will fetch a morsel of bread... And Abraham hastened to the tent, to Sarah... And Abraham ran to the herd... And he took butter, milk, and the calf which he had dressed..."? When R' Dimi came, he said, "the soul found no purpose in the body except for what is alluded to here in the matter of sacrifices. Even if the sacrifices are no longer brought, the Torah persists...."*

The Zohar continues with a Talmudic analyzed previously, that studying the passages concerning the sacrifices can make up for not offering them. The Zohar then continues:

> *Rabbi Krusp'dai said, he who verbally recites the matters of the sacrifices and their accouterments in the synagogues and study halls and has intent, it is guaranteed that those angels that recall his sins, to his detriment, will only be able to do good to him. Who will prove this? This section. It says, "and behold, three men were standing over him [alaw]." What does* alaw *really mean? They were investigating him. When that righteous man's soul saw this, what does it say? "He ran to the tent." What is the tent? The study hall. And what does it say? "Quick, prepare three measures of fine flour." This is the nature of the sacrifices. The soul finds direction through them, and this is what "and Abraham ran to the herd" means.*

That is, in the Zohar, the Torah's description of Abraham's vision of his interaction with the angels is a sacrificial ritual, just like the Covenant Between the Parts (Genesis 15) was an intricate sacrificial ritual. Similarly, the incidents described in Judges 6 and 13, wherein Gideon and Manoah, respectively, offered to prepare "meals" for their angelic visitors, are also descriptions of sacrifices. Just like our prayers are brought before the Throne of Glory by the ministering angels, so too, the parts of the sacrifices burned on the altar are brought heavenward by the fire, and this is what the verses mean when they describe the angels as "eating." As Psalms 104:4, says, "[You] make winds Your angels, the flaming fire although corrupted, Vilna version of the Mishneh Torah, in which the above law says, "anyone who offers the Pesah on a private altar is liable for lashes" in the present tense instead of the past tense. It is therefore clear to us why Maimonides would not include this law in his list: It was only temporary, and not meant forever. But we still need an explanation as to why, of all the various laws that applied during the periods when *bamot* were allowed, which can be found scattered throughout the Talmudic literature but mostly at the conclusion of Z'vahim, and which he analyzed in his commentaries, Maimonides recorded only this one. And, to return to the point where this discussion started, we have to account for what the source verse means in context, prohibiting sacrificing the Pesah on a private *bama* even after the construction of the Temple, when sacrifice at the *bamot* became completely forbidden, forever.

In his commentary to Deuteronomy 16:2-6, Rabbi S.R. Hirsch writes:

> *Even though there already was a prohibition [to offer any sacrifice outside of the Temple], it was necessary to repeat this prohibition when concerning the Passover offering. After all, the Pesah is the sacrifice that establishes the home and the family.*

In other words, the plain meaning of the passage is that because all Jewish adults, including women and slaves who are normally exempt from the other holiday sacrifices and other time-bound positive commandments, must offer the Passover sacrifice, and it is connected to many matters of home and family: it was to be eaten in familial groups, and its laws convert the house into a sanctuary, and the commandments of the seder night need the active participation of the children, and in its historical instance, it was actually offered in private residences outside of the land of Israel, perhaps one would reason that the Passover offering may be sacrificed on a private altar. The verse thus teaches that it must still be offered in the Temple. In addition, Maimonides included the esoteric understanding of this verse before detailing all of the various rules regarding the Pesah, the rules that emphasize the connection of Passover to the Jewish home and family, stressing that even when the argument for offering it on private altars was stronger, when private altars were lawfully and regularly utilized, it was not to be done.

The ensuing Talmudic discussion notes the inconsistency in this Mishna, first saying that the Pesah is the only distinction, and then giving a whole class of distinctions. The Talmud answers that the Mishna means that the Pesah and any sacrifice similar to it are to be offered on the public *bama*. In the original language, it can possibly be inferred that the Pesah's rule is the precedent and legal source for the similar rule that applies to the other sacrifices that are similar to it.

Maimonides formulates his ruling, or more accurately, his historical synopsis, thusly (The Passover Offering 1:2-3):

> *The Pesah may only be slaughtered in the Temple Courtyard, like other sacrifices. Even when sacrifice at the* bamot *was permitted, the Pesah would not be offered on a private altar. Anyone who would have offered the Pesah on a private altar would have been liable for lashes as if he offered it in the marketplace, as Deuteronomy 16:5 states, "You shall not be able to sacrifice the Passover offering within any of your gates which the Lord your God gives you." According to the Oral Tradition, it was taught that this is a warning not to slaughter a Pesah on a private altar even during the period when sacrifice on the* bamot *was permitted.*

Now, the Sefer Hahinnuch counts this law as a prohibition in its own right, as one of the 365 negative commandments, while Maimonides does not count this law as one of the 365 negative commandments. Noting this, the Minhat Hinnuch wrote (Commandment 487):

> *Maimonides and the rest of the counters of the commandments did not count this law as a negative commandment in its own right... That is all in the past, and the* bamot *will never again be permitted, and it is also known that Maimonides would not include [in the Mishneh Torah] any rules that have no practical consequences. It must be that he believes that [ever since the* bamot *became prohibited] whoever sacrifices the Pesah outside of the Temple violates this additional injunction aside from the general prohibition against all sacrifice. The contrary seems reasonable in my humble opinion. Why didn't Maimonides count this as a negative commandment?*

Rabbi Kappah has pointed out that the Minhat Hinnuch had the classic,

> *there is only one place suitable for sacrifice, and therefore a period when* bamot *are prohibited.]*

According to the initial assumption, Rabbi Simon made a distinction between the historical periods before the building of the Temple, when *bamot* were permitted, and after the building of the Temple, when *bamot* became forbidden forever, but it follows that if there is a Temple, there is also a general prohibition of any sacrifice outside of the Temple.

> *Now when is this [Pesah performed]? If we say, after midday, [which is the requisite time of day for the Pesah], let him even incur excision too [for violating the general prohibition of certain sacrifices on* bamot*]! Hence It must surely mean before midday.*

However, it should be interpreted that Rabbi Simon was only speaking about the time before the building of the Temple, and what he meant was that even then there were specific days and hours when certain sacrifice was still forbidden:

> *No: in truth it means after midday, but it means the period when* bamot *were permitted. But surely he says, 'When* bamot *are prohibited'? — He means when the* bama *was forbidden for that [Pesah], but permitted for another[, non obligatory sacrifice].*

He distinguishes between the morning of the fourteenth of Nisan and the afternoon thereof. If somehow one were to have offered his Pesah that morning, it would be considered an ordinary peace-offering, which would be permissible on a private altar, but it would not count toward his paschal obligation. In any event, he would not have violated any prohibition.

The general rule regarding what was offered on private *bamot* and what was offered on the single, public *bama* is in the Mishna (Megilla 9b):

> *There is no difference between a great [i.e., public]* bama *(a reference to the altar of the Tabernacle) and a minor [i.e., private]* bama *except with regard to the Passover sacrifice. This is the general rule: Any offering brought as a vow or as a freewill-offering may be offered on a minor* bama*, however, that which is not a vow or a freewill-offering may not be offered on a minor* bama.

VIII. Korban Pesah and the High Places

Deuteronomy 16:2-6:

> *You shall sacrifice the Passover offering to the Lord your God, of the flock and of the herd, in the place which the Lord shall choose to cause His name to dwell therein... You shall not be able to sacrifice the Passover offering within any of your gates which the Lord your God gives you, but rather at the place which the Lord your God shall choose to cause His name to dwell therein, there you shall sacrifice the Passover offering...*

In context, this commandment to not sacrifice the Pesah outside of the Temple is seemingly redundant. The previous chapters of Deuteronomy had mentioned the general prohibition of all sacrifice outside of the Temple, and served as the source for the historical circumstances that existed during the times of Joshua's conquest, Samuel's ministry, and the reigns of Saul and David when the sacrifice of personal offerings on *bamot*, "high places," private altars, was permitted even though the original Tabernacle built by the Israelites when they left Egypt served as the place of central, public worship. Indeed, some of the medieval commandment-counters, including the Sefer Hahinnuch, count this prohibition as an independent commandment, thus implying that one who sacrifices his Pesah at a *bama* violates two prohibitions. Others, like Maimonides, do not count this as a separate commandment, but then must account for the apparent redundancy. We can thus summarize the first question: What is the novelty of this injunction against sacrificing the Pesah anywhere other than the Temple?

There is a teaching that appears in a number of Talmudic sources, and here we will analyze the account that is the most detailed (Z'vahim 114b):

> *Rabbi Simon said: How do we know that one who sacrifices his Pesah at a private* bama *when* bamot *are prohibited, violates a negative command? Because it is said, "you shall not be able to sacrifice the Passover offering within any of your gates." You might think that it is also thus when* bamot *are permitted; therefore it is stated, "within any of your gates." I have told you [that he violates a negative commandment] only when all Israel enter through one gate [i.e. when*

says: 'In the evening,' you sacrifice; 'at sunset,' you eat, and how long do you continue to eat? Until 'the appointed time of your departure from Egypt,' (i.e., the morning of the fifteenth of Nisan).

We see here that with regard to eating the Passover sacrifice, the verse in Deuteronomy is explicitly understood to be referring to sunset, and not some later time, for if it were, it would have to add some other expression, like *w'taher*, or "the stars came out" to indicate that. This point is also clear from reading Rashi's combined commentary to this verse and the Talmudic passages. The fact that we now have two verses that make it clear that the Passover offering and the matza may be eaten before nightfall might explain why Maimonides and others did not consider the competing opinion, making an implicit allowance.

What then is forbidden during the latter half of the afternoon on the fourteenth of Nisan? According to the Rosh, the Tosafists, and the Shulhan Aruch, one can still eat *matza ashira* (and in some cases matza-meal products,) until the second half of the afternoon, and after that he can still eat fruits and vegetables and the like, but according to Maimonides, the Zohar, and the Vilna Gaon, all forms of matza are forbidden the entire day, and once the second half of the afternoon hits, one should no longer eat anything, but he has the option of accepting the holiday early and beginning his seder and Yom Tov meal even before the stars come out.

In conclusion, there is much justification for starting Passover and the seder early, especially for those who have difficulty waiting until late just to start the seder. Although he likely disagrees in this particular case, R'abbi Hershel Schachter has taught us that every stringency leads to a leniency. Many more children and the elderly can be much more active participants at the seder and stick around for more of it if we were to take advantage of the straight halacha and avoid the stringency in this case. That is, one who is strict with starting his seder after nightfall is acting leniently regarding those weaker individuals' fully participating, while one who is lenient in this regard allows more to participate in the seder.

commandments. Just like accepting the Sabbath early is not obligatory while Yom Kippur must be accepted early, so too there is an obligation to eat matza the first night of Passover, while there is an additional option to continue performing the commandment of eating matza until the twenty-first of the month, the end of the holiday.

Further, there are a verse and corresponding Talmudic passages that indicate that the commandment to eat the meat of the Passover offering may also begin before the stars come out, although apparently only after the sun sets. On the very first folio of the Talmud, the sages are looking for a scriptural source for the distinction between sunset and nightfall, when the stars come out (B'rachoth 2a-b):

> *"Uva hashemesh, and when the sun sets, w'taher." The sunset is a necessary condition for [the priest] to eat t'ruma, but no atonement offering is necessary to enable him to eat t'ruma. But how do you know that these words "and when the sun sets" mean the setting of the sun, and this "w'taher" means that the day clears away? It means perhaps: "And when the sun [of the next morning] appears," and* w'taher *means the man himself becomes pure? Rabba bar R' Shila explains: In that case, the text would have to read* w'yit-har. *What is the meaning of* w'taher? *The day[light] clears away, as the expression goes, "The sun has set and the day has cleared away."*

That is, for the halachot under discussion, the emergence of the stars is sometime after sunset, when the daylight has left the sky. Later, we read (B'rachoth 9a):

> *[The argument between] these Tannaim is similar to the argument of other Tannaim in the following* baraitha: *"There you shall sacrifice the Passover-offering* ba'erev, *in the evening,* k'vo hashemesh, *at sunset,* mo'ed, *at the appointed time, of your departure from Egypt." (Deut. 16:6) R' Eliezer says: "In the evening," you sacrifice;*

R' Eliezer points out that in this verse, 'erev is used in the sense that we use nowadays when we say "erev Shabbos," Friday afternoon as the Sabbath approaches.

> *'At sunset,' you eat [the sacrifice]; 'at the appointed time of your departure from Egypt' you must burn [the remaining meat]. R' Joshua*

Therefore, according to the approach used by the Shulhan Aruch in other places, there is not necessarily an obligation to eat the matza and Passover offering specifically after the stars come out. One only needs to eat them once the holiness of the day is accepted. Further, even if one were to accept the argument that the matza of the seder needs to be eaten after nightfall, it does not follow that the cups of wine also be consumed after nightfall. The idea of the Terumat Hadeshen, that even the Kiddush preceding the matza must be recited after nightfall, is not one that can be found in the Talmud, and was unknown to many of the Rishonim.

There is a verse that seems to support the contention that the holiday of Passover can be accepted before nightfall, and then one can begin to perform the commandment of eating matza. The source for the basic concept that any Sabbath or Yom Tov can be accepted early is the verse (Leviticus 23:32), "on the ninth of the month in the evening, from evening to evening, observe your sabbath," a reference to Yom Kippur, which is observed on the tenth of the month. The sages teach us that one is to begin observing the practices of Yom Kippur while it is still technically the ninth of Tishrei by accepting Yom Kippur late in the day. Most then apply this concept to any sabbath-like day, while Maimonides, according to the Vilna Gaon, believes that while doing so is obligatory regarding Yom Kippur, it is "merely" optional and meritorious to do so for other holy days. Now, if you look at Exodus 12:18, parallel language is used to describe the commandment to eat matza: "In the first [month], on the fourteenth of the month in the evening, eat matzot, until the twenty-first day of the month, in the evening." (This parallel is even more striking in the Hebrew, which is almost verbatim.) Once again, the reference is to the holiday which actually begins on the fifteenth, implying that just like the observance of Yom Kippur begins while it is still Yom Kippur eve, Passover, and the explicit commandment to eat matza, also begin on the fourteenth, as the day wanes. Ironically, a single phrase is taken out of this verse, "in the evening, eat matzoth," to prove that the matza must be eaten when it is unmistakably evening, after nightfall.

Elsewhere, this verse is used as the source for the Vilna Gaon's idea, alluded to above, that there are obligatory commandments and optional or even eat the matza. Their alternate view not only seems to have been shared by the majority of Rishonim, it was the practice up until the modern era, because of the difficulty engendered by a world without electricity.

The first issue is about the key word, *shetehshach*. As you can find in all other contexts, *shetehshach* literally means "when it gets dark," and the onset of darkness is used to designate the line between the ordinary day and the holy day, or vice versa. This is how we understand it with regards to accepting the Sabbath, reciting the Kiddush, and then eating the meal. It so happens, that according to Maimonides, for example, the standard of "nightfall" is specifically with regards to the list of Talmudic laws above, which do not involve the performance of positive commandments that require a specific holy day, but with regards to commandments that are prescribed for a particular day, like the Kiddush and meal on the Sabbath and on the festivals, or eating the matza on Passover, once someone has accepted the holiness of the day, he can perform those commandments.

As for the sources that explicitly declare that the matza and sacrificial meat must only be eaten at "night," they are not saying "night" as opposed to the time that is "day," i.e., when the sun is shining, but rather "night" as opposed to the times when other sacrificial meat may be eaten. Other sacrificial meat may be eaten the day it is slaughtered, and then the ensuing night, and sometimes the ensuing day also, without interruption. The Pesah, unlike all the other sacrifices, cannot be eaten on the calendar day it is slaughtered, the fourteenth of Nisan, and it must not be left by the morning of the fifteenth. By "night," the sages were saying that only the night of the fifteenth of Nisan is the time for eating the Pesah, but technically the night starts once the festival is accepted.

In answer to the Rosh's argument that the Mishna did not need to rule that one should begin to build up an appetite in advance of Passover, and therefore the Mishna meant that the eating of the matza and Pesah literally be after nightfall, other Rishonim believe that the Mishna is specifically forbidding all foods, not just forms of *path*, because every form of *path* is either already forbidden as a form of leaven, or forbidden as a form of matza.

This opinion, that Kiddush should not be recited before dark, is based on a number of Talmudic sources that mention that the consumption of the Pesah is to be done after *tehshach*, or specifically at night, as opposed to day. The Rosh and the Tosafists understood that this certainly applies to the meat of the offering, and it could be seen from the Tosefta that the same applies to the matza, which was eaten in conjunction with the Pesah. Now, one has the opportunity to accept the holiness of the Sabbath or Festival even before the sun sets, and on those days, he may also recite Kiddush and have his meal well before nightfall. This opinion would still allow for one to accept the festival early and recite Kiddush and begin the seder early, just as long as the eating of the matza eventually is done after nightfall. Considering that *maggid* intervenes, it is not too hard to do so. However, there are also authorities, like the Terumat Hadeshen, who link even the rabbinical commandments of the evening with the eating of the matza, and therefore, the drinking of the first of the four cups also has to be after nightfall.

The Rosh has an interesting argument: It is well known that one should avoid eating *path*, the ancient term that included all types of bread, whether leavened or unleavened, or baked goods that were not bread but were halachically treated like bread if one were to make his meal of them, in the latter half of the afternoon before any Sabbath and Yom Tov so that he has an appetite when the holy day starts, so why does the Mishna in P'sahim specify that one should also avoid eating before Passover "before it gets dark?" It must be that the Mishna is emphasizing that the meal that starts Passover is different from all other holiday and Sabbath evening meals, which may be conducted even before nightfall. The Passover meal has to be later. (There is an opinion that even if one accepts another Sabbath or Yom Tov early, his meal has to extend to the time after the stars come out, but in most places this stringency is not followed.)

The Shulhan Aruch's method of deciding between conflicting opinions makes this ruling not fully consistent with other halachot, as there is also the unaddressed opinion of the Rif and Maimonides and others (the Tosefot Harosh, for instance), who disagree on a number of points, and who did not recommend waiting for nightfall in order to recite Kiddush

activities. And, unlike any other sacrifices, the participants could not eat the Pesah the day it was slaughtered, but rather, had to wait until the night, which is halachically the next day, to eat it. Normally, it is not only permissible to eat of a sacrifice on the very day it is offered, it is even meritorious. Rather, we could suggest that with regards to all of the other sacrifices, the ideal time to eat them is the daytime. Thus, those who are, for example, to bring their holiday pilgrimage offerings on the first festival day, the fifteenth of Nisan, bring their offerings on the morning of the fifteenth. However, because the Pesah is meant to be eaten on the night of the fifteenth, they could not wait for the following morning of the fifteenth to slaughter it! In other words, because the Pesah is bound to the night of the fifteenth, it is specifically slaughtered after the regular service of the fourteenth is concluded in order to show that it is meant for the following "day," and if not for the fact that the Temple is closed at night at and no sacrifices are then brought, we would have thought to offer it then.

VII. When is the Earliest Time One May Start the Seder?

The Shulhan Aruch (Orah Hayim 472:1) rules that

> *One should have his table set while it is still day so that he can eat immediately* k'shetehshach, *when it gets dark, and even if he is in the house of study, he should rise [to do so] because it is a commandment to hurry and eat [the matza, maror, and paschal lamb] before the children fall asleep, but he should not recite Kiddush until* shetehshach, *it gets dark.*

The common understanding of this passage is that "dark" refers to a time usually identified with *tzeith hakochavim*, when three stars become visible, which is somewhere between a quarter and a third of an hour after sunset, and perhaps even slightly earlier. This is explicitly defined by the Talmud as the time when 1. the evening *sh'ma* may be recited, 2. priests who had immersed during the day are considered ritually clean enough to eat *t'ruma*, and 3. when the Sabbath and Yamim Tovim officially end. For our purposes, we will refer to this moment as "nightfall."

There are situations whereby the positive commandments do not override the negative ones, and commandments performed in the Temple are in that category, and therefore the positive commandment to eat of the Pesah does not override the commandment to not break the Pesah's bones. Notice that this selection from the Talmud, which is the accepted halacha, assumes that the act of consuming the Pesah offering takes place in the Temple. However, it is also certain that the Pesah is actually never eaten within the Temple. By the time that it is to be eaten, the Temple is closed for the night, and the meat must be eaten within a building in the residential part of Jerusalem, within the city walls. The Talmud thus considers the house hosting the consumption of the Passover offering, even if in Egypt, as a *de jure* Temple for these intents and purposes.

The sages also taught us that an individual Pesah may only be eaten by those who had registered in advance, and it is the individual's responsibility to make sure that he is registered with a group before its designated animal is slaughtered. The language used in the Torah is "a lamb for each father's house, a lamb for a house," as typical groups consisted of large extended families, and the sages assumed that certain close relations could register family members without their explicit knowledge. Once again, this rule is unique to Passover, for with regard to other similar sacrifices, once again for example, the thanksgiving offering, any Jews who are ritually pure can join in the consumption even if they had not pre-registered. However, once again, this law is analogous to a law of the priesthood, whereby the Temple service was divided among large extended families, called *mishmarot*, "watches," on a weekly basis, and every day of the week was the turn of a group of priests from that watch to serve in the Temple, and they would not allow other priests to take part in that day's service or to eat of that day's sacrifices. Similarly, the weekly showbread was only apportioned to the priests whose watches began and terminated on that particular Sabbath.

The Pesah is also unique in that it is offered after the daily afternoon public lamb offering, the *tamid*, is offered, whereas there is a general rule that on any given day, any animals must be offered only after the morning burnt lamb and before the afternoon lamb, which was normally the public signal that the priests were preparing for the end of that day's "*b'etzem hayom hazeh*, on that very day the Lord took the Israelites out of Egypt." Our sages say that "God calculated the end" and the night of the Exodus was, according to the verse, "*leil shimmurim*, a guarded night." The Exodus happened at exactly the right time, not a day late or early. The *'etzem* was preserved, and in commemoration we also preserve the *'etzem*. This also explains why this commandment was only recorded after the Exodus, because this facet of the Redemption was only realized after the Pesah was consumed.

With this in mind, we can now add two more halachic sources for the idea that the Jewish home is considered a sanctuary, especially when it hosts the consumption of the Passover offering.

Z'vahim 97b:

> *Rava said: a positive commandment does not override a negative commandment in the Temple.*

Normally, a positive commandment of the Torah does override a negative commandment. For example, the act of circumcision involves actions that would be considered forbidden labors on the Sabbath, but when the positive commandment to circumcise a child presents itself, it overrides the commandment not to perform the forbidden labor. The Gemara continues:

> *For it was taught [regarding the Passover offering]: "neither shall you break a bone thereof." R' Simon ben Menassia said: [This refers to] both a bone which contains marrow and a bone which does not contain marrow.*

That is, if someone needed to obtain a morsel of marrow in order to fulfill his commandment to eat the offering, he might reason that he could violate the commandment not to break a bone of the sacrifice in order to get that marrow. Yet, the prohibition wins in this case. The Gemara concludes its proof:

> *Why so? Let the positive commandment come and override the negative commandment! You must thus infer that a positive commandment does not override a negative commandment in the Temple.*

The meat of the sacrifice must also be eaten as one becomes satiated, and, as we saw above, within the defined boundaries of its "place." These rules do not apply to the meat of any other similar offerings. Rather, when one would, for example, consume the meat of a thanksgiving offering in Jerusalem, he was not bound by any rules dictating where in Jerusalem that meat had to remain, nor did it matter how much of it each individual would eat and whether he had reached satiety. However, as can be seen in T'mura 23b, similar regulations do apply to the priests who eat of the holier sacrifices within the Temple courtyard: the meat may not be removed from the courtyard, and if it has been removed, it becomes disqualified, and the priests are to eat their portions to the point of satiety. The consumption of the Pesah meat is elevated to a level of stringency normally only applied to that of the priests within the Temple, because the Passover transforms its participants into priests, so to speak, within their own private domains.

As for the injunction against breaking the Pesah's bones, I have not found an analog among the laws of the sacrifices, but I can offer something else. On the verse (Exodus 13:46) which first mentions the prohibition, Rashbam says that the bones should not be broken "with [the sacrifice] eaten in haste," but he cannot have been referring to the original sacrifice as eaten in Egypt, because this commandment was given after the Exodus, and more tellingly, applies to all future generations, who would probably not be eating their portions in anticipation of leaving Egypt. Similarly, there was and is no eternal commandment to eat the Passover with our "loins girded and our staves in our hands." It must be that Rashbam is referring to an idea intrinsic to the consumption of the sacrifice. As we saw before, the Pesah represents God's compassion and salvation, while the matza represents our haste and enthusiasm for leaving the exile, to take a leap of faith into His hands across the great wilderness. The Rashbam is saying that the prohibition against breaking the Pesah's bones is meant to remind us what the Pesah itself represents, and that we not confuse its message with that of the matza, which represents the haste of departure.

On a deeper level, we find that the Hebrew word for "bone," *'etzem*, occurs in the same passage of the Torah but with an alternate meaning,

Talmudic support. Secondly, the entire idea of *derech heruth* is rabbinic, and is the impetus for the rabbinic laws of reclining at the seder and drinking four cups of wine, but the prohibitions enumerated above are all biblical. Thirdly, the Talmud records an implicit reason for eating the Pesah roasted and not cooked (P'sahim 41a):

> *Our Rabbis taught: "Do not eat of it raw, nor any form of boiled with water." I only know [that it may not be boiled] in water; how do we know [it may not be cooked in] other liquids? You can argue a fortiori, if water, which does not impart its taste, is forbidden, then other liquids, which do impart their taste, should all the more so be forbidden.*

This passage shows us that the Sages believed that the reason for these two commandments was to preserve the true and pure taste of the Pesah, and this fits well with the idea that the consumption of the Pesah has to be done in a way that allows for the internalization of the unadulterated lesson of the sacrifice.

As for the prohibition of removing meat of the offering from its place, Maimonides writes (9:3):

> *Meat of a Pesah that has left its group['s place], whether intentionally or inadvertently, becomes forbidden for consumption. It is like the meat of the most holy sacrifices that left the [Temple] Courtyard or the meat of the less holy sacrifices that left Jerusalem's walls, which are both like non-kosher meat, which carries the penalty of lashes for its consumption...*

This halachic analogy assumes that with regards to the meat of the Pesah, the Jewish house stands in the place of the Temple, and the consumption of the Pesah therein by the Jewish family is akin to the consumption of the sacrifices by the priests within the actual Temple.

Thus, we can continue the equation. The meat of the Pesah may not be left over, just like the priests are enjoined not to leave over any meat for consumption beyond its allotted time, and the priestly portions of the sacrifices may not be eaten by priests who have served idols or who are uncircumcised, or by those who are non-priests.

VI. The Detailed Laws of the Passover Offering

In light of all this, we can better understand some of the other commandments of Passover.

According to Torah law, the paschal lamb must be eaten roasted, and there are many prohibitions related to the consumption of the meat:

It may not be eaten "cooked or partially roasted," i.e. prepared in any way other than roasting.

The meat may not be left over by the next morning.

The meat may not be fed to a non-Jew,

a renegade Jew,

or an uncircumcised Jew.

The meat of a particular paschal sacrifice may only be eaten by those who had pre-registered to eat of it before it was slaughtered.

The meat may not be removed from the house in which it is being eaten by the group.

One may not break any of the sacrifice's bones.

The sages further instituted that nothing be eaten after the paschal lamb, "so that the taste stays."

Considering the principle that the Pesah is specifically meant to be eaten, as opposed to the other sacrifices, we can easily understand this rule of the Sages: the eating helps internalize the lesson, one which is to last the entire night, and that is why "the more one tells about the Exodus, the more praiseworthy," another commandment the greatest sages fulfilled until morning.

The Sefer Hahinuch offers a reason for some of the above-enumerated prohibitions. It is *derech heruth*, "the way of free men," and the practice of princes to eat meat roasted and not cooked, and they do not worry about leaving some for a later meal, nor do they break the bones of their portions while attempting to find every last morsel of meat. However, his theory has some issues. Firstly, it does not enjoy any scriptural or

food of slaves that needed to be baked even before the Exodus, while the matza of the end of Maggid, the whole matza, represents the haste that we showed when we left Egypt, when another batch of slave food was prepared not because it was slave food, but because there was no time to allow it to rise. The matza of the sandwich represents our active demonstration of hastily leaving the exile and going home to the land of Israel. The maror, of course, represents the bitterness of the bondage, but in the sandwich, it only makes the meat and bread, the deliverance and Exodus, taste better.

So, what if the metaphorical and physical sandwiches of redemption lack the meat, the aspect of God's compassion which is shown by our ability to offer the sacrifices? No sacrifice means no Temple and no service, which mean that we are still undeserving of God's complete mercy. If we were deserving, we would merit to have the Temple and the Passover offering. But they are missing. All we have is a rushed, bitter-lettuce sandwich that represents leaving the bitterness of the exile. So what can we do? We should add matza. Enough matza to make up for the missing offering. If we want the restoration of the Temple, we have to show that we are doubling our efforts to leave the diaspora. We double up on matza and the haste to leave the fleshpots of Egypt and America. And that, God willing, will lead us to be able to have a complete seder.

V. Kimha D'fischa

We can thus understand why the alms usually collected in advance of Passover have been colloquially referred to as Kimha D'fischa, or "Passover flour" in Aramaic. Giving charity is a year-round commandment, and more so before the festivals, but we have not seen, for example, that the funds collected before Sukkot were ever given their own moniker, like "sukka money" or "*esroig gelt*," or the like. Rather, it seems that because these funds were for the express purpose of buying the flour from which to bake the matzot that would replace the Passover offering, they were called "Passover flour," i.e., "the flour that stands in place of the Passover [offering]."

of replacing the Pesah with something that needs to be eaten, we have to look at the nature of the Pesah. Technically speaking, the Pesah is the only form of sacrificial meat that a Jewish person must eat. A person can go his entire life without eating from any other sacrifice if the need never arises, but he cannot avoid the Pesah. So much so, that eating the Passover offering is only one of two positive commandments that must be performed on the penalty of excision, the other being circumcision. That is, one who does not eat of the Passover offering is as deserving of punishment as one who does not circumcise himself, or one who desecrates Yom Kippur. Further, the purpose of the offering of the Pesah is fundamentally different from that of all the other sacrifices. While the main purpose of the other sacrifices are the portions that are offered on the altar, the "satisfying aroma," the Pesah's main purpose is the ritual eating of the meat. Yes, to qualify as a sacrifice, its blood and fats need to be placed on the altar, but the commandment is that the meat be eaten at the seder as part of the educational process, and therefore when there is no meat something else should be eaten.

But why matza? I found one line in the classical works that sheds light on the question. After entertaining the idea that perhaps maror should be eaten instead of or along with the matza of *afikoman*, Rabbi Joel Sirkis, the author of the commentary called the Bayit Hadash on the Tur, offers that matza was the chosen replacement because it is both a commandment and "it is in memory of freedom, just like [the meat of the] Pesah." I hope that the elaboration is as follows:

Rabban Gamliel says that whoever does not mention three components of the seder has not fulfilled his obligation to tell the story of the Exodus: Pesah, matza and maror. These three foods represent facets of the miracles of the Exodus, and all are to be eaten. Rabban Gamliel's grandfather, Hillel the Elder, believed that they all must literally be eaten together as a sandwich, although the rest of the Tannaim, as well Maimonides, ruled that such may not be done. The Pesah represents that God "passed over" our houses in Egypt, an anthropomorphism which Onqelos translates as "He took compassion" on us. That is, the meat of the sandwich represents God's active salvation. The matza of the beginning of the seder, the broken matza, represents poverty and oppression, and was the

Most importantly, we have the concept of studying the sacrifices (M'gilla 31b):

> *Abraham said before the Holy One, blessed be He: Master of the Universe, perhaps God forbid, Israel will sin before You and You will do to them as You did to the generation of the Flood and the generation of the Dispersion? ... This is very well for the time when the Temple stands, but when there is no Temple what will befall them? He replied to him: I have already fixed for them the order of the sacrifices. Whenever they will read the section dealing with them, I will reckon it as if they were bringing me an offering, and forgive all their sins.*

This idea is reflected in many more Talmudic passages. When we know we cannot offer the sacrifices, we instead recite and study the relevant biblical and Talmudic passages that describe the sacrifices. This is the basis for the daily recitation of the korbanot before the morning (and afternoon) services, and the musaf prayers. The practice of the Vilna Gaon was to recite all the relevant passages the afternoon of the 14th of Nisan, which was the time for the bringing of the Passover offering.

One would therefore conclude that instead of eating something at the seder when the time comes to eat the Passover sacrifice, we should read a relevant biblical or mishnaic passage that describes how the action would and should be done.

So, the question remains, why eat something? We never do that when we cannot offer some other sacrifice. We don't do that for the other sacrifice, the Hagiga, that is also missing from the seder! Further, assuming that we will therefore eat something at the seder to replace the missing Pesah meat, why would it be matza? Eating matza is its own commandment that we have already fulfilled. Why should we replace this missing mitzwa with one that we have already performed? Strangely enough, the sages of the Talmud make both assumptions, that something should be eaten in memory of the Passover and that it should be matza, and they only argue about how that matza should be eaten, with maror or without, or that maybe all of it should be eaten in one shot at the conclusion of the meal.

I would like to suggest answers to these questions. As for the necessity

in memory of what was and will be. The biblical commandment to eat maror is only applicable when the Pesah is present, so in its absence we have the rabbinic commandment to eat maror even when we cannot eat the sacrificial meat. Further, the seder plate is really supposed to have the meat of both the Pesah and the Hagiga, the additional festival peace-offering on it, but in the absence of those sacrifices, we place a piece of roasted meat and a roasted egg on the plate in their memory. And there are many other rituals that we follow that are in memory of what was and should be, including, according to many, the counting of the Omer, which the sages enacted in memory of the true count as prescribed by the Torah for when the Temple is standing.

But sacrifices should be different. We have a general rule that if a sacrifice's time has passed, the sacrifice has been missed (B'rachoth 26a), i.e., we do not seek to make up sacrifices that have set times that were missed. If we did not bring the daily lamb offering this morning, there is nothing we can do but make sure to offer any subsequent sacrifices on time. (Sacrifices that are imposed on individuals due to their circumstances, such as those imposed upon women who give birth and converts upon their conversion, must be brought no matter how late, so when the Temple service is restored every convert will have to bring a sacrifice even decades after his conversion, and every woman will have to bring a number of offerings corresponding to her births.) If we missed the time for offering the paschal lamb, there is nothing we can do to replace it. Further, the sages imposed a rule that roasted lambs and kids not be eaten the first night of Passover (B'rachoth 19a):

> *Theodus of Rome had the Roman [Jews] eat whole roasted kid goats on the night of Passover. Simon ben Shetah sent to him and said: Were you not Theodus, I would excommunicate you, because you make Israel [appear to] eat holy foods outside [Jerusalem].*

Maimonides and the Shulhan Aruch rule likewise, and most communities have a further custom against eating on the night of the seder any roasted meat that is not from an offering. If there is no sacrifice, we should not do something that looks like we are eating sacrificial meat in a forbidden place.

by Maimonides thusly (Laws of First Fruits, 3:14):

> *The first fruits require* lina. *How so? Once one has brought his first fruits to the Temple, made the declaration, and offered his peace offerings, he should not depart from Jerusalem that day to return to his place. Instead, he should stay there overnight and return to his city the following day, as it says, "you shall turn around in the morning and go to your tents." Any time you turn to leave the Temple once you go there should be only in the morning.*

That is, when one brings any sacrifice to the Temple, he has to stay within the confines of Jerusalem, the annex of the Sanctuary which is designated for the consumption of the sacrificial meat, that night, even if he has already finished consuming the meat, and the paschal service is the case from which the rule is derived for all other offerings.

Thus, in Egypt, the Israelites were similarly commanded to remain within their houses the night they ate the Pesahim, precisely because their houses had been sanctified as the sanctuaries and places of consuming the holy food. They stayed home until morning because the law of *lina* applied to the Pesah even in Egypt because the Jewish home has always been a model sanctuary.

IV. The Importance of Eating on Passover, and Why Replace the Offering with Matza?

According to the Talmud (P'sahim 119-120), when the seder is lacking the meat of the Pesah, we are to eat a second portion of matza in its stead. Although the word *afikoman* refers to some sort of dessert that one may have wanted to eat after eating the sacrifice, the word eventually came to refer to this second portion of matza that is put aside at the start of the seder to be eaten after the holiday meal. Various laws and customs that apply to the meat of the sacrifice were then transposed to this portion of matza: it has to be eaten in order to complete one's satiation, nothing can be eaten after it, and it needs to be eaten by dawn (or midnight to play it safe), just like the actual Pesah, and there are a number of familiar features of the seder that are also

That is, as we learn from the first chapters of Leviticus, the altar's main function is to receive the application of the blood from the sacrifice, and this is also the main rite that effects the atonement from any sacrifice. In Egypt, the Israelites had no sanctuaries or high places, so they needed some place to perform the Korban Pesah. After all, if there was no altar and no component of the offering placed on the altar, in what sense was the consumption of the lamb in their houses considered sacrificial?

In light of what we mentioned above, that the tent of the patriarchal families, and by extension, the Jewish home, stood in the place of the Sanctuary before there was a sanctuary, we understand why the doorways stood in for the altars. The Israelites could not place altars even a few feet from their pitiful hovels, because the sanctity and purity of the Jewish home did not extend into the unclean Egyptian street, but as we see, the altar is meant to stand in the open area in front of the entrance of the true Sanctuary. Thus, only the doorway, which was just beyond the home but not yet in the street, took the place of the altar. (This idea may be alluded to in the original Hebrew expression used to describe the altar as, "the altar that is at the entrance to the Tent of Meeting," which is actually missing a word describing where the altar is in relation to the tent, and can be read "the altar that **is** the entrance of the Tent of Meeting." Often, Onqelos does not translate this phrase literally, but rather as "the altar that is **in the courtyard** of the Tent of Meeting.")

With this in mind, we can understand that in Egypt, the Israelites had to stay within their houses the night of the service of the Passover offering just as they would stay overnight in Jerusalem centuries later. In Deuteronomy, Moses describes the eternal commandment to offer the sacrifice in the Temple (16:7):

You shall cook and eat [it] in the place that the Lord, your God, will choose, and you shall turn around in the morning and go to your tents.

To which Rashi brings a rule found in a number of places in the Talmud:

This teaches that [the pilgrim] is required to remain [in Jerusalem] overnight until the Yom Tov is over[,]

a law known as *lina*, lodging overnight in Jerusalem, which is formulated

Israelites were instructed to stay within their houses all night:

> *This tells [us] that once the destroyer is given permission to destroy, he does not discriminate between righteous and wicked. And night is the time that destroyers are given allowance...*

I always found this explanation insufficient. The sages, starting with Onqelos in his translation, explained that it was not literally the blood on the doorpost that saved the people, but rather the merit of the performance of the commandment that saved the Israelites, just like it does not literally mean that God passed over anything, but rather that he took compassion on the people. That is, staying in the house did not necessarily protect them, and the sages even mention that if an Egyptian firstborn attempted to hide himself in an Israelite house that night, he was still smitten. Further, why were all the people bidden to remain inside all night if only the firstborns had what to fear? As we will see later, the firstborn male Israelites were only about 20,000 out of 600,000, and the firstborn women may have constituted a similar fraction. Also, the sages say that all of the firstborn were killed exactly at midnight. By some hours later, the Egyptians, including Pharaoh, were out in the streets trying to drive out the Israelites, and say, by 3 o'clock or so they would see that all those out in the streets were not miraculously dying. By an hour or two before sunrise, it should have been safe for the Israelites to begin to leave their houses in order to reach the rallying point from which they would make their exodus.

All of these issues lead me to interpret this verse along the lines of the Mechilta's commentary to the earlier verse wherein God originally gave Moses the commandment to apply the blood of the Pesah to the doorways, 12:7:

> *And they shall take [some] of the blood and put it on the two doorposts and on the lintel, on the houses in which they will eat it.*

To which the Mechilta adds:

> *We thus learn that they had three altars in Egypt: the two doorposts, and the lintel. Rabbi Ishmael says they were four: the basin, the two doorposts, and the lintel.*

universal center of organized prayer, pilgrimage, sacrifice, and divine revelation. This explains why it was also Abraham's practice to erect altars "and call in the Name of the Lord" (i.e., to pray and preach) wherever he would encamp.

On the moral level, we see that the Jewish home, which is the continuing legacy of the home of Abraham and Sarah, is meant to be a sanctuary. Rabbi Avigdor Miller wrote much about this aspect, and it is sufficient to say that of course one should not bring any detestable or impure object into the home. This helps us understand another aspect of marriage (Sota 17a):

> *Rabbi Akiva expounded: When a husband and wife are worthy, the Divine Presence abides with them; when they are not worthy, a fire consumes them.*

In light of what we saw earlier, we can suggest that the Divine Presence abides with a couple because they turn their home into a sanctuary, and if they misuse their relationship, it can cause destruction, similar to the misguided worship involving the Golden Calf. Further, just like Maimonides rules that "the High Priest is greatly revered" (Temple Appointments 5:3), a man should also treat his wife, the high priestess of the home, with exceptional respect.

III. Lodging Overnight in the Egyptian Sanctuary of the Exodus

As part of the ritual of the paschal offering in Egypt, Moses instructed the people (Exodus 12:22-23):

> *You shall take a bundle of hyssop and immerse [it] in the blood that is in the basin, and apply the blood that is in the basin to the lintel and to the two doorposts. As for you, no one shall go out from the opening of his house until morning. The Lord will pass to smite the Egyptians, and He will see the blood on the lintel and on the two doorposts, and the Lord will pass over that opening, and He will not let the destroyer enter your houses to strike.*

Rashi and other medieval authorities bring a midrash to explain why the *places it [in its designated] place [of consumption].*

We thus see that the Passover offering must be eaten within a defined place, and that place, a private building or house within Jerusalem, becomes the meat's "place of consumption," similar to the rule that the priests have to eat the meat of the holier sacrifices within the defined area of the Temple courtyard. This commandment and its laws seem to turn the house hosting the seder into a kind of sanctuary, alluding to the state that existed in the times of the patriarchs, before there was a sanctuary or tabernacle. But first an explanatory digression:

Where have we seen that our sages described female, Jewish high priestesses?

In regards to the matriarchs Sarah and Rebecca (Genesis 24:67):

> *Isaac brought her to the tent of his mother Sarah, and he took Rebecca, and she became his wife, and he loved her. Isaac was comforted for [the loss of] his mother.*

To which Rashi brings the paraphrased words of the Midrash (Genesis Rabba 60:16):

> *I.e., she became the likeness of his mother Sarah, for as long as Sarah was alive, a candle burned from one Sabbath eve to the next, a blessing was found in the dough, and a cloud was attached to the tent. When she died, these things ceased, and when Rebecca arrived, they resumed.*

Rashi omits the aspect that the doors of the tent were also open to all, i.e., that all who were needy were welcome, which appears in the original version of this midrash. The miracles that took place in Sarah's tent are reminiscent of those that took place in the Temple: the western lamp of the menorah burned constantly, the showbread was sufficient to satiate all the priests, the Temple served as a house of prayer for all peoples, and the cloud of God's Glory hovered over the Temple.

We can learn a number of lessons from this.

On the historical-theological level, we see that the house of the fathers served in the capacity that the Sanctuaries would later serve, i.e., as the

So Moses (33:7):

> used to take the tent and pitch it beyond the camp, far from the camp, and he called it the tent of meeting. It would be that anyone who sought the Lord would go out to the tent of meeting which was beyond the camp.

That is, the Divine Presence as manifested by the prophet bearing God's word was too awesome to remain among the people, and needed to be kept far from their habitation. Thus, only once Moses had spent another 40 days on the mount achieving forgiveness for the people were they able to learn how to build a proper meeting place for mortals and the Divine within the middle of their camp.

This could also be a reason for the refrain, "as the Lord commanded Moses," that ends more than two dozen of the verses at the conclusion of the book of Exodus describing the construction of the Tabernacle in practice. The Israelites' previous attempt to create a tangible locus for approaching the Divine was completely out of consonance with God's word; this attempt was exactly as He had commanded.

With regards to the rebuilding of the Temple, we see that God commanded us to build a temple for Him and to offer Him sacrifices therein, and despite the inherent dangers, we must do all that we can to fulfill those commandments, and it is thereby that we will merit to receive the Divine Presence in our midst.

II. The First Principle: The Jewish Home as a Sanctuary

Maimonides writes:

> The 123rd [negative] commandment is the injunction against removing the meat of the Passover offering from the place in which [the assembled] had gathered to eat it, as He has said: "You shall not take any of the meat outside," (Exodus 12:14) and in the words of the Mechilta, "outside – outside of the place of its consumption." It is forbidden to eat that which does leave, and it is treated like any other non-kosher meat. In Tractate P'sahim they said: One is only liable for removing meat of the Passover offering from group to group once he

> *Now, why should we die by letting this great fire consume us? If we continue to hear the Lord our God's voice, then we will die. For is there any mortal who has heard the living God's voice speaking out of the midst of the fire, as we have, and lived?*

But they did not wish to be entirely distant. God granted the people's request that Moses act as the intermediary, but then, when they built the Calf using the same wisdom that would later be properly used to build the Ark of the Covenant, they made a critical error that Bezalel would not make (B'rachoth 55a):

> *R' Samuel bar Nahmani said in the name of R' Johanan: Bezalel was so called on account of his wisdom. At the time when the Holy One, blessed be He, said to Moses, "go and tell Bezalel to make me a tabernacle, an ark, and vessels," Moses went and reversed the order, saying, "make an ark, vessels, and a tabernacle." Bezalel said to him: "Moses, our teacher, as a rule a man first builds a house and then brings vessels into it, but you say, make me an ark, vessels, and a tabernacle. Where shall I put the vessels that I am going to make? Perhaps the Holy One, blessed be He, said to you, 'make a tabernacle, an ark, and vessels?'" Moses replied, "perhaps you were in God's shadow and knew!"*

Bezalel realized that first the housing for such a powerful machine as the Ark had to be built. The Tabernacle had a courtyard surrounding it, and it was guarded by the Levites and Aaronites. The Tent of Meeting itself was multilayered, and admittance thereto was highly restricted. The Calf, however, was made straight away, without any levels of separation between it and the people, and in great haste. When the rabble-rousers declared, "These are your Gods, O Israel," the Calf led to a spiritual meltdown within the people's camp.

Once Moses had destroyed the Calf, God told him (Exodus 33:5):

> *Say to the children of Israel, "you are a stiff-necked people; if I were to go up among you for just one moment, I would finish you. Therefore, take your ornaments off of yourselves, and then I will know what to do to you."*

After the first Divine Revelation at Sinai, the people asked that Moses serve as the conduit for God's word unto the people (Deuteronomy 5:23):

"You should approach and hear all that the Lord our God will say, and you shall speak to us all that the Lord our God may speak to you, and we will listen and do."

The Cherubim that adorned the Ark of the Covenant were also by no means idols; they were actually a complicated machine that acted as a divine receiver and speakers for God's word, and a gauge of closeness of the people to God. Similarly, the Midrashim discuss how the Golden Calf was made to move and speak, as though it were a machine similar in function and mechanics to what the Cherubim would be. However, the Cherubim had been divinely ordained, whereas the Calf was a grave error.

Rashi comments on the rays of light that shone from Moses's face (Exodus 30:34):

Come and see how great the power of sin is, for when they had not yet stretched out their hands to sin, what does He say? "The appearance of the glory of the Lord was like a consuming fire at the top of the mountain before the eyes of the children of Israel" (Exod. 24:17), and they were neither frightened nor quaking, but once they made the Calf, they even recoiled and quaked from Moses's rays of splendor.

Here, then, is how we understand the succession of events:

Divine revelation is as a devouring fire. It is powerful and dangerous. There are many ways that modern electric power plants can be built, but the plants that use nuclear energy have to be built especially well, with super-thick, reinforced concrete walls to prevent the lethal radiation from leaking out. Building a nuclear power plant like a coal-burning plant or like a hydroelectric plant would present a major danger to mankind and the environment.

Similarly, the extreme holiness of the divine presence must be carefully kept from frequent and direct human contact. The people realized this early on, when they said (Deuteronomy, *ibid.*, 21-22):

A Treatise on the Esoteric Meanings of the Passover Commandments.

I. The Tabernacle and the Golden Calf

Bringing the Passover offering requires access to the Temple, from which we have become distant due to our sins. Today, some argue that we should continue to stay away from the site of the Temple because of its halachic and physical dangers. There is a precedent for this argument, but there is also a rejoinder.

We will begin this analysis with a discussion of the circumstances surrounding the building of the Golden Calf. The sages make it very clear that the Golden Calf was not intended to be an idol or a deity; rather it was meant to be an intermediary between the people and God, a replacement for Moses (Exodus 32:1):

> *When the people saw that Moses was delayed in coming down from the mountain, the people gathered themselves together to Aaron, and said to him, "Get up, make us a god who will go before us, because this man, Moses, who brought us up from the land of Egypt, we know not what happened to him."*

they were less likely to be leavened. In truth, heavily leavened dough can also be made into crackers, while fresh, unleavened dough can be baked into soft cakes.

Maror and Haroset:

Maror is any of five vegetables described by our sages as qualifying for use in fulfilling another biblical commandment to be eaten along with the Korban Pesah. In the event that the Korban Pesah was unavailable, the sages decreed that maror be consumed regardless. Haroset is a dip made of fruit, wine, and nuts. The sages ordained that maror be dipped in the haroset before being consumed.

Karpas:

any other non-maror vegetable. However, the common name "karpas" reflects the classic custom to use celery, which is called "karpas" in Aramaic and "karfas" in Arabic.

Kiddush and Wine:

Kiddush is a set of blessings recited on a cup of wine to mark the onset of a Sabbath or a Holiday. The sages used to dilute their wine with water. This practice persisted even in the days of Maimonides and the Shulhan Aruch, the latter ruling that even a cup that is 25% wine and 75% water is considered halachically wine. The sages also recognized that although grape juice is inferior to its alcoholic product and should not be used for sacrifice, it is still halachically wine and may be used for the four cups.

A Note on the Terminology.

In order to make this haggada accessible to the wider community which has experience with traditional Passover seders that have been conducted in the last few centuries but little to no experience with the way the seder was meant to be conducted, I thought it would be important at the outset to define the terms that come up most often.

Korban Pesah (or sometimes just "the Pesah," plural Pesahim):

a sacrifice that the Torah commands each and every adult Jew to bring to the Temple on the fourteenth of Nisan. It can be either a male lamb or goat in its first year, and many people can register to eat of one animal together, as long as it provides enough meat for every participant to receive a minimum of an olive's volume of its edible meat for consumption at the seder on the ensuing first night of Passover.

Matza:

unleavened bread. The Torah commands that every adult Jew consume at least an olive's volume of matza the first night of Passover, and according to some authorities, it is a continuing voluntary commandment, as opposed to an obligation, the rest of the holiday. Matza, like leavened bread, can come in any form, as long as its dough was baked before it had a chance to rise. It is a common misconception that matza must be in cracker form, or that some classic decisors preferred crackers because

is that this haggada be used when Passover arrives, as by then, the classic haggada that has been used until now will be, in the most fortunate way, in need of an update.

This haggada is based on the traditional Ashkenazi text of the haggada, but incorporates the main Maimonidean rulings regarding the conduct of the seder, because most of the classical Ashkenazi authorities did not express their opinions regarding the laws of the Seder if done in the ideal manner, i.e., in Jerusalem with the Passover offering. I ask the reader to please note the color-coded changes in wording that reflect the fact that the Passover offering and the Temple are no longer distant memories, but rather realities.

It should be noted that even when we do bring the Passover offering, those who do not come to Jerusalem to participate in the sacrifice, due to their inability to travel or their having become ritually contaminated in a way that prevents them from participating, or for whatever other reason, will still use the classic haggada because they will conduct their Seders as we have been doing in years past. I pray that those in this category will be a small minority.

Most importantly: Practical experience with the laws of the sacrifices and ritual purity and impurity is very uncommon, and there is little room in this volume for giving a sufficient overview thereof, and therefore, those who wish to participate in bringing and/or eating the Passover offering should thoroughly familiarize themselves with the relevant laws, as this haggada will only address matters directly related to the Seder.

I hope that Haggadat Hapesah will lead to further research into the laws of Passover, the Temple, and the sacrificial service, and that it serves as a wake-up call for the Jewish community the world over.

May it be the will of He who dwelleth in Zion that we merit to celebrate Passover together in Jerusalem, and that with His help, this haggada will be the only one that future generations recognize.

persists until today and is worthy of a thorough and comprehensively researched understanding.

Our generation has witnessed both the beginning of the third Jewish commonwealth and the ingathering of the exiles, and more and more of our people are growing interested in the study of the Temple and the sacrificial service, and there are even deliberations in the Knesset concerning the right of Jews once again to worship on the Temple Mount. Also, when the sages discussed the Omer, the offering of the new barley grains on the second day of Passover, which would permit the people to begin to consume the new crop, they assumed that the Temple, which was in ruins right before the holiday, would be speedily rebuilt, as though literally overnight, and fully functional on the first day of Hol Hamo'ed. Therefore, when the Temple will be rebuilt, we will be unprepared for the halachic requirements and consequences of conducting the sacrificial service. When the greatest of commentators, Rashi, considered this discussion in light of the prohibition against building the Temple at night and on the Sabbath and festivals, he concluded that the future Temple would miraculously descend from heaven, complete and ready for the service. Other commentators believed that it would not be so, as there is a biblical commandment that the Jewish people themselves build the Temple, and they understood the Talmud to be describing a situation whereby the ongoing construction of the Temple would be completed on Passover, the finishing touches, as it were, or that the sacrificial service would be renewed on Passover, while the construction of the rest of the Temple would take some more time. Indeed, this idea has the strength of historical precedence. The Torah explicitly describes how the sacrificial service, for example, began at the Sinaitic revelation under the care of the firstborn males, and continued on a daily basis until the Tabernacle was inaugurated and the service was made the domain of the Kohanim of Aaron's family. Similarly, altars were set up on Mount Moriah and sacrifices were brought thereon in advance of the construction of both the first and second Temples. Therefore, it seems clear from all of this that we too should be prepared for the relative suddenness of the renewal of the sacrificial service, and that it is our duty to prepare for it.

Therefore, it is imperative that we also prepare a corpus of literature to be used that day when, God-willing, the service is renewed, and my intent

Introduction:

Why Create a New Haggada?

The classic text of the Passover haggada developed some time after the Jewish people stopped bringing the Passover offering in the wake of the destruction of the Second Temple, although some have speculated that a minority continued to bring the Passover offering even after the destruction of the Second Temple. According to the Mishna, the primary focus of the Seder is the consumption of the meat of the offering, and without it, the Seder retains only a shadow of its ancient glory. Many of the salient features of the Seder have been fixed by our sages to act as substitutes or memorials to what was and what it is supposed to be. A good example would be what we know as the afikoman, a portion of matza that is set aside to be eaten towards the end of the Seder, thereby taking the place of the Passover meat.

Many are under the impression that, from a halachic standpoint, we cannot offer sacrifices today. However the truth is that despite the unfortunate state of the Temple, all of the laws governing its sanctity are still in effect, and technically, the sacrifices may still be brought even though the Temple edifice has yet to be built. However, we have not brought the Passover offering, or any offering for that matter, in the intervening centuries due to political considerations, a situation that

HAGGADAT HAPESAH
הגדת הפסח

Rabbi Avi Grossman

בס"ד   **מכתב ברכה**   הרב שלמה חיים הכהן אבינר
                                ראש ישיבת עטרת כהנים

ב"ה, ה' אלול תשע"ג

לכבוד גורן

יישר כח

על דברי שלך להוסיף שיעורים

על גידולו של ילדינו על כפיו

יזכו לגדל ילדיהם בתורה ביראה

ובגדולה, נעים, לארץ, למדינה, לעולם, (לאורים)

אוהב אתכם

בס"ד

מכתב ברכה

הרב דוב ליאור
רב העיר
קריית ארבע היא חברון ת"ו

בס"ד, יז סיוון תשע"ט

מכתב ברכה

הובאה לפניי הגדה של פסח מאת הרב אב"י גרוסמן. עברתי על חלק מהחיבור ושמחתי לראות יצירה חדשה שנראה שלא קיימת כמותה. על הגדה של פסח נכתבו פירושים יותר מעל כל דבר אחר, אך המיוחד בהגדה זו שהיא משלבת בתוכה את הציפייה הגדולה של כלל ישראל לראות בהתחדשות עבודת בית המקדש על כל המשתמע מכך.

אין ספק שחזון רוחו של הרב המחבר וציפייתו הגדולה לעתיד המקווה, נותנים כוח להכין את הלבבות לקראת קיום המצווה בהגיעה שעתה.

יישר כוחו של הרב המחבר, ויהי רצון שיפוצו מעיינותיו חוצה ויזכה לקרב את ישראל לאביהם שבשמים.

החותם לכבוד התורה ולומדיה,

דוב ליאור

מכתב ברכה

הרב משה צוריאל
בני ברק

בס"ד

מכתב ברכה

להופעת הספר "הגדה של פסח" עם הערותיו של הרב אב"י גרוסמן

למדונו חז"ל שהעולם קיים על שלשה עמודים, תורה, עבודה וגמילות חסדים (אבות א). במלת "עבודה" כוונת חז"ל לעבודת הקרבנות. חשיבות הקרבנות כבר מבוארת ע"י מהר"ל בספרו "גבורות השם" (תחילת פרק ס"ט). ובזמן חז"ל ראש כל התפילות היה שיבנה הקב"ה שוב את בית מקדשנו.

"כל שיחתן של בריות אינה אלא על הארץ. 'עבדת ארעא', 'לא עבדת'. וכל תפלתן של בריות אינה אלא על הארץ. 'מרי! תעביד ארעא. מרי! תצליח ארעא'. [אבל] כל תפלתן של ישראל אינו אלא על בית המקדש. 'מרי! יתבני בית מקדשא. מרי! מתי יתבני בית מקדשא?'" (בראשית רבה יג, ב).

בדורות אחרונים נחלשה בקשה זאת, חלק מפני לחצים פוליטיים וחלק מפני שהחינוך המודרני נתלש מהמקורות.

ברוך יהיה הרב אב"י גרוסמן שהחזיר עטרה ליושנה. הוא השתמש בהההדרת "הגדה של פסח" עם פירוש מעניין שלו במבט מיוחד לצרף אל האמירה ההלכות הנוגעות להקרבת קרבן פסח, וביאר בהרחבה במבוא של עשרים עמודים כמיהה נפשית זו, עשיר בהפניות למקורות חז"ל וראשונים.

כל בן תורה ישמח מאד במהדורה זו של "הגדה של פסח", כי ליד כמה קטעים בה מצוין באופן תמציתי ההלכות, עם קשר רעיוני להקרבת הקרבן.

על חשיבות קרבן פסח, ראו במהר"ל (בספרו "גבורות השם", סוף פרק שלושים וחמשה). הקרבן הוא אבן יסוד לבניית עמנו.

אשרי הרב גרוסמן שהלהיב את הלבבות במעשה אומן זה, שחיבר הספר בדייקנות ובחֵן מושך-לב.

החותם,
הרב משה צוריאל
מחבר: "לקט פירושי אגדה" ועוד ספרים רבים

א' אדר ב, תשע"ט

בס"ד   # מכתב ברכה   אוריאל ספז
                                                         רב הישוב כוכב יעקב

3/12/19   ה' אדר ב, תשע"ט

ברכה לרגל הוצאת הגדת הפסח

באתי בזאת לברך את הרב אבי גרוסמן, מישובנו כוכב יעקב, שזכה להוציא לאור את חיבורו החשוב על הגדה של פסח הנוהגת בזמן המקדש, שיבנה במהרה בימינו אמן.

כל מי שיקרא בספר יווכח לגאונות של המחבר ואף על מקוריות המחשבה.

רציתי להוסיף שתי הערות:

1. אנו מייחלים לבניית המקדש בצפייה רבה, ואנו יודעים שכל ההדרכות בנושאים הללו יבואו ממרכז ההנהגה התורנית בעם ישראל, שהיא הסנהדרין. בשלב המקדים עד שתקום הסנהדרין, אנו מקבלים הוראות מהגוף שקם בכינוס כל גדולי ישראל, בזמן מרן הראי"ה קוק שהיא הרבנות הראשית לישראל.

2. הרבה מנהגים השתרשו בעם ישראל במהלך הדורות. לא תמיד אנו יורדים לעומקם של דברים, ולכן עלינו להיזהר להוקיר ולכבד את המנהגים שנהגו בהם גדולים בינוניים וקטנים.

אחד המנהגים הוא פתיחת דלת הבית לפני אחד מהם הוא אמירת 'שפוך חמותך על הגויים....' הבא לבטא את הרצון שלנו לראות בנקמת ה' שצרו לישראל במהלך כל הדורות. ושמעתי על הרב צבי קוק שהיה אומר אותו בקולי קולות ובתפילה לה' יתברך שיגלה את מלכותו עלינו במהרה ותיראה חביבות שלו כלפינו.

אני תפילה שיזכה המחבר, להוציא עוד ספרים, ויזכה לכוון לאמיתה של תורה.

בברכה אוריאל ספז
רב הישוב

פל': 052-7204557   פקס: 02-9974016   Sfez12@gmail.com

David Lau
Chief Rabbi of Israel
President of the Great Rabbinical Court

דוד לאו
הרב הראשי לישראל
נשיא בית הדין הרבני הגדול

בס"ד, ו' כסלו, תש"פ
4 דצמבר, 2019
הסכ' - 121.שפ

לכבוד
הרב **אברהם בן יהודה גרוסמן** שליט"א

מכתב ברכה

מידי שנה יוצאים לאור עולם פרשנויות נוספות על "הגדה של פסח". ארון הספרים מכיל בתוכו עשרות אלפי ספרים שמטרתם לבאר את ההגדה.

מיוחדת היא **"הגדת הפסח"** שאתה מתעתד להוציא לאור עולם. הגדה זו מיוסדת על הלכה למעשה כיצד יש לקיים הקרבת קרבן פסח כהלכתו וכיצד סדר פסח יתנהל כשעילה הרצון מלפניו יתברך ונזכה לקיימו כראוי. הרי אם נצליח להקריב קרבן פסח במועדו וכהלכתו נוסח הסדר פסח ישתנה, ויפה כינסת את הדברים והבאת לאור עולם סדר פסח כשקרבן הפסח הוא במרכזו.

בעניין הקרבת קרבן פסח בזמן הזה האריכו רבים, וראיתי לנכון להביא את דברי הגר"ד מקארלין בספרו "שאילת דוד" בקונטרס "דרישת ציון וירושלים" שדן בשאלה האם ניתן לתקן להקריב קרבן פסח בימינו, בתנאי, אם המקום קדוש קדוש לעתיד, כשיטת הרמב"ם שמקריבים גם כשאין בית המקדש, יהיה הקרן הקדש לקרבן פסח, ואם המקום אינו קדוש השחיטה תהיה חולין וזריקת דם כזורק מים בעלמא והקטרה כשורף חלב בעלמא. וראה בדבריו שמכריע וז"ל: "אך לא נוכל לעשות זאת לדעת הרמב"ם מכמה דברים וספיקות" עיי"ש בדבריו.

וראה בשו"ת רבי שלמה אליעזר אלפנאדרי (סי' טו) שכתב שגם לפי דעת הרמב"ם שמותר להקריב קרבנות אף שאין בית המקדש, בכל אופן לא מצאנו בתקופות התנאים שהיו בירושלים אחר חרבן הבית שהקריבו קרבנות למרות שיכלו להקריב בטהרה. ויש להאריך בסוגיא זו, ואכמ"ל.

אצטט את דבריו של בעל שו"ת שערי צדק (הרב מנחם מנדל פאנט, או"ח צו) שדן בשאלה זו הקרבת קרבן פסח בזה"ז, ומסקנתו: "אמנם בעיקר הדברים אי אפשר להקריב בזמן הזה. נ"ל לפרש "ומפני חטאינו וגו' מפני היד השלוחה" וגו' הענין דקאמר "אין אנחנו יכולים" וגו'. אף שיתנו לנו רשות, אסור לנו להקריב מפני היד, והיינו משום ששמו שקוציהם בביהמ"ק, וגם עתה היא כן וכמ"ש קצר המצע מהשתרע, ואיך אפשר שבמקום ביהמ"ק נקריב בצד א' לשם שמים ובצד השני יעשו מנהיגיהם והיינו היד השלוחה במקדש ממש". והדברים מדברים בעד עצמם.

ואסיים מעין הפתיחה, דבריך ערוכים בטוב טעם ודעת ושופכים אור על אפשרות שבע"ה נזכה לה במהרה בימינו אמן, לאכול מן הפסחים ומן הזבחים בקדושה ובטהרה.

מברכך בכל לב

דוד לאו
הרב הראשי לישראל
נשיא בית הדין הרבני הגדול

for their help and guidance, first and foremost the Mara D'atra, Rabbi Uriel Sfez, and Rabbis Zvi Pereg, Mordechai Rabinovitch, Moshe Gozlan, and Meir Attar, the founder of Tomer Devorah Institutions, and his wife, Rebbetzin Rhonda, for all of their advice and generous support. This work would not have been possible without the help of Rabbi David Avihayil, Rosh Yeshivat Ramot, and Rabbi Moshe Zuriel, Rabbi David Bar-Hayim, and Avremi Raanan. There are no words to describe their immense contributions to this project. I, and the entire Jewish community, are indebted to Rabbi Eliyahu Weber, the head of Yeshivat Hamikdash, for his thorough review of this work, and for his dedication to the rebuilding of the Temple and the renewal of the sacrificial service.

This English translation of Haggadat Hapesah was made possible through the generous support of our dear friends, Dr. Simon Daniel and family of Woodmere, New York, and our dear neighbor, Mr. Michael Belote. May they always merit to be among those who use this haggada every Passover.

I am personally and eternally grateful to Rebbetzin Bat-Hen Grossman, who has worked for years so that I could be free to study and research to my heart's content. She served as this haggada's designer and layout artist. May God reward her in both this world and the next, and may we merit to celebrate many more Passovers together.

In Appreciation

Our sages ordained that we recite the Hallel when the Korban Pesah, the Passover offering, is slaughtered in the Temple courtyard on the fourteenth of Nisan, during the Passover Seder the following night, and on the morning of the next day, the first day of Passover. It should be noted that in the Torah itself, Hag Hapesah, the Passover festival, is always a reference to the fourteenth of Nisan, the day we refer to as Passover Eve, whereas what we refer to as Passover, the seven-day festival which starts on the fifteenth of Nisan, is invariably referred to as Hag Hamatzot, the Festival of Unleavened Bread. On the former festival, the Levites serving in the Temple courtyard would ultimately recite the Hallel several times. We thus see that in our sages' view, Passover is a time dedicated to praise and thanksgiving. Accordingly, I would like to thank God for granting me the precious time to complete this haggada, so that we may learn how to keep the commandments according to His will and live to celebrate many more holidays and festivals.

I would like to thank my parents for everything they have given me in this world. My esteemed father, Mr. Jonathan Grossman, served as the editor of this English edition of Haggadat Hapesah, and deserves special credit. I would also like to thank my in-laws for both raising my wife and their constant support these last fifteen years.

I would like to express my gratitude to the rabbis of Kochav Ya'akov

In Loving Memory of our grandparents,

Emerich & Jean Schwartz

Abraham & Marsha Grossman

Yehuda Gez

Yehuda Leon & Naomi Ninio

Yankel Jacque & Etla Ridnik

and my late cousins

Benzion Yishai Nulman

and Shmuel Berman

לזכר נשמת

שיינדל בת דוד ואסתר שרה

יצחק אייזיק בן יעקב הכהן ומינדל

אברהם בן חיים וריסא

מאשא חיה בת אשר ודבה רייכל

יהודה בן ר' אליהו וג'ולי

נעמי בת שאול וחנה

יהודה בן שמואל ודונה

אטלה בת יוסף וחנה

יעקב בן אליהו וגולדה

בן-ציון ישי בן עזרא לייב ופנינה

שמואל בן ראובן איתן

לזכר נשמת

The English Translation of Haggadat Hapesah has been made possible by the generous support of Dr. Simon and Ariella Daniel, and is dedicated by them in loving memory of their grandfather,

Mr. Jack Poolat
יעקב אליהו בן רחמים

who passed away on 22 Siwan, 5773
May 31, 2013.

May his memory be for a blessing.

HAGGADAT HAPESAH
A Torah L'Maaseh Publication
By Rabbi Avi Grossman
Kochav Yaakov, Israel
054-675-4962
avrohom.grossman@gmail.com

הגדת הפסח
מאת הרב אב״י גרוסמן
הוצאת תורה למעשה

ISBN 9789655983463
© Copyright 2021, 2023 Rabbi Avi Grossman
All rights reserved.

כל הזכויות שמורות לפי דין תורה ולפי החוק הבינלאומי לרב אב״י גרוסמן

Haggadat Hapesah has been made possible by the generous support of:

Mr. and Mrs. Jonathan Grossman	Shlomo Fisherowitz
Rabbi Hanoch & Naomi Gez	Yigal Saperstein
Dr. Shmuel & Ora Ninio	Binyamin Lemkin
Mrs. Malka Gez	Joel Sklar
Eli & Malki Ninio	Isaac Moses
Marcos & Dorit Dana	Rabbi Gil Student
Jagay & Sarit Dana	Lisa Herman
Yoav & Chana Gez	Rabbi Aharon Assaraf
Shimon & Michal Gez	Rabbi Koby Milgraum
Osnat Fried	Neal Frohlich
Rafi Hecht	Ayala Ben Menachem
Yosef & Chedva Kaplan	Rabbi Yonatan Friedman
Hillel & Chava Kovacs	Rabbi Israel Weinstock
Akiva & Devorah Montal	Netanel & Efrat Arbeli
Yaacov & Hila Prupis	David Aaronson
Rabbi Amichai & Sara Leah Gez	Dani & Sima Rubin
Dr. Yona & Dr. Lilach Saperstein	Rabbi Ben Keil
Barry & Mindy Spielman	Dr. David Krausz
Moshe & Edie Nulman	Benjamin Greenblatt
Dr. Yaakov Friedman	Louis Gordon
Michael Grossman	Daniel Kaganovich
Yoni Harris	Avi Kessner
Chaim Gottesman	Rabbi Dr. Jeremy England
Michael Rollhaus	Lisa Liel
Mrs. Mona Montal	Ari Leifer
Dr. Daniel Berman	Abshalom Meiri
Naomi Adams	Rabbi Moshe Gozlan
Barry Silbergleit	Rabbi Eliyahu Maimon
Daniel Baum	Rabbi Eliyahu Sharvit and family
Rabbi Reuven Berman	Mr. and Mrs. Moshe Flatzman
Saul & Susan Grossman	Mr. and Mrs. Casriel Accardi
Dr. & Dr. Ranon Udkoff	Mr. Jack Shama

HAGGADAT HAPESAH
הגדת הפסח

Rabbi Avi Grossman

Haggadat Hapesah is part of an ongoing series.

The sequel, Hall'luhu B'theqa Shofar, is already in print, and can be purchased from Torah L'Maaseh publications, and another two sequels are on the way.

Much time and effort goes into the production of these important books. To help support their production and publication please visit:

https://www.patreon.com/rabbiavi
https://www.gofundme.com/f/haggada

Thank you.

For more materials, check out Rabbi Grossman's blog at www.avrahambenyehuda.wordpress.com and his videos at https://www.youtube.com/@MachonShilo1

Friend Rabbi Avi Grossman on Facebook at www.facebook.com/rabbiavigrossman